Desire and Decline

Society and Politics in Africa

Yakubu Saaka
General Editor

Vol. 13

PETER LANG
New York • Washington, D.C./Baltimore • Bern
Frankfurt am Main • Berlin • Brussels • Vienna • Oxford

Frances Vavrus

Desire and Decline

Schooling Amid Crisis
in Tanzania

PETER LANG
New York • Washington, D.C./Baltimore • Bern
Frankfurt am Main • Berlin • Brussels • Vienna • Oxford

Library of Congress Cataloging-in-Publication Data

Vavrus, Frances Katherine.
Desire and decline: schooling amid crisis in Tanzania / Frances Vavrus.
p. cm. — (Society and politics in Africa; 13)
Includes bibliographical references (p.) and index.
1. Education—Social aspects—Tanzania—Case studies. 2. Education—
Tanzania—Public opinion—Case studies. 3. Postcolonialism—Tanzania—
Case studies. I. Title. II. Series.
LC191.8.T29 V38   370'.9678—dc21   2002040648
ISBN 978-0-8204-6311-7
ISSN 1083-3323

Bibliographic information published by **Die Deutsche Bibliothek**.
Die Deutsche Bibliothek lists this publication in the "Deutsche
Nationalbibliografie"; detailed bibliographic data is available
on the Internet at http://dnb.ddb.de/.

The paper in this book meets the guidelines for permanence and durability
of the Committee on Production Guidelines for Book Longevity
of the Council of Library Resources.

Printed in Germany

To Hallie and Gus Vavrus

My first teachers
My finest teachers

Contents

List of Illustrations ix

List of Tables.. xi

Acknowledgments xiii

Introduction   Education and the Postcolonial Condition 1

Chapter 1   International Development and the
                 Feminist Modern... 25

Chapter 2   Transformations in Schooling in
                 Northern Tanzania 45

Chapter 3   "Condoms Are the Devil" and the Culture-
                 as-Cure Conundrum....................................... 65

Chapter 4   AIDS and Education in an Era of
                 Economic Decline... 89

Chapter 5   "The Water Is Ours": Commodities, Community,
                 and Environmental Conservation........................... 109

Chapter 6   Postcolonial Interventions in Education, AIDS,
                 and the Environment 133

References... 153

Index... 165

Illustrations

Map 1   Tanzania Administrative Districts and
Major Cities.. xvii

Map 2   Moshi Municipality, Old Moshi, and the
General Location of Schools in This Study............. 11

Figure 1   Students at Mbali Primary School in 2002
Putting on a Chagga *Ngoma*, a Drum and Dance
Performance 50

Figure 2   Blackboard at a Private Secondary School
After an English Lesson 76

Figure 3   Secondary School Girls Preparing for an
Examination 95

Figure 4   Mr. Muhubiri Demonstrating the Action
Block Press to Mr. Moshi.. 140

Tables

Table 1   The Model of Schooling Used in Tanzania................... 3

Table 2   Summary of the Research Process............................... 19

Table 3   Number of Public and Private Secondary
               Schools in Mainland Tanzania (1994) and
               Census Population (1988) 57

Table 4   Student Enrollment in Public and Private
               Primary and Secondary Schools, 1961–1994........... 62

Table 5   Household Resources in Mainland Tanzania,
               the Kilimanjaro Region, and Among
               Secondary School Students in the Study,
               1996 Questionnaire.. 98

Table 6   Data on Contraceptive Use from the 2000
               Questionnaire 103

Table 7   Socioeconomic Profile of Four Primary
               School Communities, 2000 119

Table 8   Educational Profile of Four Primary
               School Communities, 2000–2001 120

Acknowledgments

I am grateful to the many friends, colleagues, and family members who have helped this project grow. The seed was planted in 1988, when I had the good fortune to meet Stacie Colwell while we were graduate students at the University of Illinois. Her enthusiasm for Swahili studies, African history, and life in general has nourished me for many years. Rick Canning's contributions also began about this time, but I thank him most of all for applying his expert pruning skills to earlier versions of this manuscript.

The ideas in this book sprouted while I was a doctoral student at the University of Wisconsin. I owe a debt of gratitude to many people from my days in Madison, including Michael Apple, Mimi Bloch, Beth Grau, Andreas Kazamias, Tom Popkewitz, Tom Spear, Amy Stambach, and, especially, Bob Tabachnick. The environment on Bascom Hill helped friendships to thrive, too, and I benefited greatly from the presence of KimMarie Cole, Rick Peterson, and Deb Rothenberg. May we continue to grow wherever we are planted.

It was in Old Moshi that this work blossomed, and I have many people to thank for it: David Fleeger, Aklei Kessy, Flora Kisaka, Sarah Kwayu, the late Ramos Makindara and Mama Makilo, B. Mchau, Zaina Mshana, Fidelis Mero, Bertha Moshi, Frank Nyange, Philip Olotu and Mama Martha, and Lisa Richey. I am especially grateful to Charles Moshi for his intellectual contributions and personal commitment to this project. In addition, I want to thank the students, parents, teachers, and officials in Kilimanjaro who have given graciously of their time over the years. Those living in the village of 'Miti,' in particular, have shown my family and me great hospitality.

To my surprise, as a kid from the cornfields of Indiana, I have found in Manhattan just the right climate to sustain this project. My colleagues in the Department of International and Transcultural Studies at Teachers College and in the Institute of African Studies at Columbia University have provided strong support. I would especially like to thank Lesley Bartlett, Dianne Sadnytzky, and

Herve Varenne, whose various forms of assistance during my tenure have been critical to the completion of this book. The warmth generated by the students in the Program in Comparative and International Education and International Educational Development could make anyone thrive; my special thanks to Monisha Bajaj, Audrey Bryan, Philippe Hemmert, Peter Mtesigwa, and Andria Wisler for helping with this project and for sustaining it in myriad ways.

My research would not have been possible without the support of a number of different institutions. The Fulbright-Hays program sponsored my initial trip to Tanzania as part of an intensive Swahili program; a Fulbright Doctoral Dissertation Fellowship provided funding for my family and me to spend a year in Old Moshi; a Dean's Grant from the University of Wisconsin supported the writing of the dissertation; the Andrew W. Mellon Foundation and the Takemi Program in International Health gave me the resources necessary to complete a postdoctoral fellowship at the Harvard School of Public Health and two periods of follow-up research in Old Moshi, with Ulla Larsen providing unwavering support as my sponsor and mentor in the Department of Population and International Health, and a Dean's Grant for Pre-Tenured Faculty at Teachers College allowed me to return to Tanzania to share the results of this study with the participants. I am also grateful to the Tanzania Commission for Science and Technology for permitting me to conduct research in the country.

It is, however, to my family that I owe the greatest thanks. My brother, Steve, has left his ecological footprint on this work by reminding me that climate matters, even to the field of education (see Chapter 5). Mary's indelible marks reveal themselves wherever I manage to keep my posts- straight from my -isms; if it were not for her sororal guidance through the land of theory, I might not have finished graduate school. Phil and Nancy Leinbach, my in-laws, have shown their support for this project in many ways, not the least of which has been caring for the 'heirs' when I have needed to travel. And my parents, Hallie and Gus, read every page of this manuscript before it went to press to make sure that I subordinated where I meant to and conjoined where I had to. More importantly, as educators with almost one hundred years of classroom experience between them, they have shown me that a life devoted to teaching is a worthy one indeed.

Finally, I want to express my deepest gratitude to Tim Leinbach for helping this project to flower. He has been there at every moment of its unfolding and has tirelessly sustained it through both words and deeds. Oscar and Gus Leinbach have also played a very important role in this process: Only they could sense when Mom was wilting in front of the computer and needed to be showered with their hugs.

I would also like to express my gratitude to Meg McCarron, cartographer, in composing the two maps in this book. The USAID/FEWS Project and EDC International Program also deserve credit for their contributions to these data sets. Grateful acknowledgment is hereby made to the Editorial Board of *Current Issues in Comparative Education* for giving me permission to reprint portions of Chapter 1, which first appeared in 2002 (Volume 5, Number 1), as "Constructing Consensus: The Feminist Modern and the Re-construction of Gender" [Online]. Available at: http://www.tc.columbia.edu/CICE/articles/fv151.htm

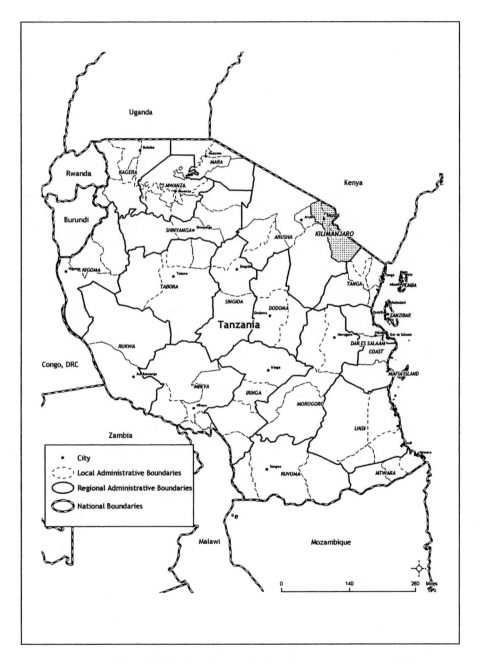

Map 1: Tanzania Administrative Districts and Major Cities

Introduction

Education and the Postcolonial Condition

Saturday afternoons were the most serene time of the week in Miti, a village of approximately 1,500 people in the Kilimanjaro Region of northern Tanzania. On the southern slopes of Mount Kilimanjaro, Miti is one of eight villages in the former chiefdom of Old Moshi.[1] There are several theories about how this chiefdom got its name (Stahl, 1964), but on those Saturday afternoons it seemed clear to me that the area was named for the steady stream of smoke— *moshi* in Swahili—that drifted from the many cooking fires. While the rest of the household took their postprandial naps, I sat on the front porch watching the smoke disappear behind the banana trees in our neighbor's *kihamba*, the ancestral garden and burial ground of Chagga families on Mount Kilimanjaro.

On this particular Saturday, I was waiting for William, one of my students at Njema Secondary School, who was coming to be interviewed as part of my research on schooling and declining fertility in the Kilimanjaro Region. William's background was similar to that of many students at Njema, a private co-educational school under the supervision of the Evangelical Lutheran Church of Tanzania (ELCT). Like most of the young men at the school, William was a boarding student because his home was in another part of Kilimanjaro. With his father in Dar es Salaam, the commercial capital of Tanzania, and his mother working in the regional capital, Moshi, William's family was also typical; the parents of many of the students live apart for most of the year because one of them—usually the father—has migrated to a larger city to find work. Although both of William's parents were employed in the 'modern' sector of the economy, he shared with his classmates from farming families the common problem of paying his school fees at the beginning of each term. Just a few weeks earlier, for instance, during the mid-year holiday, it had been announced that the national government was raising the fee cap and that this increase would be passed along to students. Although fees were already expensive enough, William and his classmates would now have to find a bit more, and on short notice, too.

As William appeared along the path through our neighbor's *kihamba*, I could see he was concerned about something. Before starting the formal interview, we drank sodas and talked about his worries: his father had not yet sent his fees for the second term, and his mother could not afford them herself. Because William was a respected student leader, he didn't think he would be sent home before his fees arrived, but his concerns about money, missed classes, and failing the national exam to qualify for university studies were common among the students I taught in 1996.

During the interview,[2] William talked at length about his role in student government and his goal of studying law at the national university. His enthusiasm for further studies, however, was tempered by numerous remarks about the difficulty of finding a job "in a country like ours," an "underdeveloped" place where employment opportunities are limited even for young people who have completed O-level and A-level studies (see Table 1). In spite of these problems, he had not lost faith in schooling. On the contrary, William argued that current conditions in the country—captured in the Swahili expression *maisha magumu*, or difficult life—called for more schooling and that people should do whatever it takes to ensure that all of their children receive, at the very least, a secondary education. "How can parents achieve this goal?" I asked him:

> *William:* Personally, I think four children is the maximum number if one's situation is good. If the situation is not so good, then two children are enough.
> *Fran:* If a man has only two children, does it mean that he has financial problems and doesn't have much money?
> *William:* It means that his problems won't be as serious as for a man with many children. Let's say that my father's salary is 40,000 shillings per month [approximately $70 in 1996], and I have to pay 40,000 just for school fees for the first term. So my father has to make sacrifices for a month to pay my school fees. Now if you have four children in secondary school and your salary is 40,000 shillings, you can't even educate one of them. They will just have to stay at home and do their own thing....I think life is more difficult now than in the past. If you take us, the residents of Kilimanjaro, as an example, we used to have very large farms. My father inherited a large farm because my grandfather had a very large farm. But he had many children among whom the land was subdivided. These children had more children, and as the number of children increased, the size of the farmland for each one decreased. Today you may wonder how we survive because there may be only half an acre to be shared among ten children. So things like this make the present situation difficult, especially for youths who have not gone to school, because they depend solely on being given farmland by their parents. The farm by itself cannot satisfy their needs, especially with crops like coffee, because the farms are small due to the population on the mountain. (interview, April 27, 1996)

Despite William's lament about the factors making life more difficult today than it used to be—population pressure, falling coffee prices, the diminishing prospects of making a living off the land—he is privileged to be one of the mere 6% of the Tanzanian population (total population 35 million) that ever attends secondary school (National Bureau of Statistics and Macro International, 2000; UNAIDS, 2002). Moreover, William's level of education far surpasses that of his parents: his mother finished Form 4, but his father completed only primary school. In addition, William lives in one of the more prosperous regions of Tanzania, the Kilimanjaro Region, with more schools, health facilities, and infrastructure than in most of the country. Yet this summary of his attainments and advantages did little to convince William that life was getting better, not worse.

Table 1: The Model of Schooling Used in Tanzania[3]

School level in Swahili	U.S. equivalent	Classes	Typical age range of students	Number in Old Moshi	Administration in Old Moshi
shule ya msingi	elementary or primary school	Standards 1–7	7–13 years old	11	public (government)
shule ya sekondari–O (ordinary) level	high school	Forms 1–4	14–17 years old	2	private (ELCA)
shule ya sekondari–A (advanced) level	first year of college or university	Forms 5–6	18–19 years old	1	private (ELCA)
chuo	college or university	1–3 years	20 years old and up	–	–

This book is an attempt to understand why faith in schooling endures, particularly in those parts of the world where social and political-economic problems seem most intractable. Why, for instance, do young people like William have such a strong desire for schooling even though it often fails to secure the jobs or the lives they desire? Why, too, do policymakers and politicians generally treat schooling as the *sine qua non* of international development regardless of the context in which it occurs? Despite countless educational interventions in recent decades, hunger, unemployment, and oppression continue in many communities in the Third World.[4] What, then, are the structural dimensions of poverty that schooling alone simply cannot redress? My goal in the following chapters is to examine the conditions that give rise to the desire for schooling among different groups of actors *and* to the conditions that constrain the transformations that schooling can produce.

Scholars in a number of fields have sought to explain the reasons for the nearly universal appeal of formal education in schools.[5] Demographers often point out that schooling, especially for females, has strong, demonstrable effects on children's health, fertility decline, and the status of women within the household (Ainsworth, Beegle, & Nyamete, 1995; Caldwell, 1998; Cleland & van Ginneken, 1988; Glewwe, 1999; LeVine, 1999; LeVine et al., 1991; Mahmud & Johnston, 1994; Mason, 1984). Indeed, one of the most well-documented relationships in the social sciences is the inverse correlation between the number of years a woman spends in school and the number of children she bears (Cochrane, 1979; Graff, 1979; Jejeebhoy, 1995).

Other scholars, notably educational sociologists and economists, have shown that the expansion of the global economy after World War II produced tremendous growth in school enrollment at all levels of the education system. For instance, in Sub-Saharan Africa, the primary school enrollment rate increased from approximately 25% in 1960 to almost 60% in 1980 (UNICEF, 1999). The expansion of schooling in Africa and elsewhere in the world has led to a striking convergence in global educational models, even though countries have vastly different social and political-economic histories (Boli & Ramirez, 1992; Meyer et al., 1977; Ramirez & Boli, 1987). These internationalized models, derived primarily from European and American school systems, have the following general characteristics: The state is responsible for most of the regulation of syllabi, tests, and teachers; classes are organized by age groups and class periods by time, and school credentials in the form of diplomas and certificates are linked to particular career paths (Schriewer, 2000). When one looks at the similarities in educational systems worldwide, it is not surprising that a global consensus has emerged on the importance of schooling. However, the vastly different conditions in which schools are situated lead not only to distinct practices inside the classroom but also to divergent possibilities outside of it.

For these reasons, some scholars remain incredulous about commonsense assumptions regarding schooling—especially for women—and development in the Third World. For instance, research by several demographic anthropologists and communications scholars calls into question the widespread belief that formal education consists of a coherent set of practices that produces remarkably similar effects for all who experience it. For example, Bledsoe and Cohen ask incisively of the demographic literature on education and fertility decline:

> How, precisely, does education work this reproductive magic? Does it teach a woman Western scientific facts about reproduction and health, instruct her in the national language in which radio messages about contraception are broadcast, expose her to ideals of low fertility, extricate her from authority of kin who demand high fertility, imbue her with career aspirations outside the home, embolden her to ask for contraceptives from intimidating family planning personnel or in the face of an irate husband? (1993, p. 89)

Additional anthropological studies demonstrate that attending school does not necessarily transform gender relations and improve women's status; instead, women with higher levels of education may experience greater domestic conflict with spouses and in-laws, and they may find themselves the victims of violence when men feel threatened by a woman's new status as an 'educated person' (Bradley, 1995; Greenhalgh, 1995; Hollos, 1991; Kumar, 1992). Furthermore, schools themselves may be sites for gender-based violence, as the murder of 19 female students by their male counterparts at St. Kizito Secondary School in Kenya illustrates (Steeves, 1997). Such examples should not deter efforts to create gender equality in schools, but they do draw attention to the fact that schooling occurs within a specific social and political-economic context that may mitigate, or even reverse, its empowering effects. The chapters in this book examine the potential for schooling to effect equality, but they look as well at the impotence of schooling alone: In the absence of a concomitant restructuring of national and international development priorities, schooling can transform very few lives.

The Postcolonial Condition

> [P]ostcolonial theory is situated somewhere in the interstices between Marxism and postmodernism/poststructuralism. It is, in a sense, but one of the many discursive fields upon which the mutual antagonism between these competing bodies of thought is played out. Seen as such, postcolonialism shifts the scene of this long-standing contestation to the so-called 'third world'.
>
> —Leela Gandhi, 1998

The state of affairs in which desire for schooling meets economic decline lies at the heart of *the postcolonial condition*. According to Gupta, this condition describes "a specific set of locations articulated by the historical trajectories of European colonialism, developmentalism, and global capitalism" (1998, p. 10).[6] Exploring the postcolonial condition in Tanzania requires delving into the ideological and material legacies of German and British colonialism; it demands attending to developmentalism—dominant representations in development discourses—to understand the appeal of educational programs for African women to solve the disparate problems of overpopulation, HIV/AIDS, and environmental degradation, and it necessitates looking at the effects of global capitalism in a specific location where many people can no longer satisfy their desire for schooling under the current conditions of *maisha magumu*. As Gandhi's epigraph suggests, postcolonialism creates a space in which to maneuver between (neo-)Marxism and postmodernism (see Chapter 1). Moreover, Gupta's framework for studying the postcolonial condition provides a way to examine how colonialism, developmentalism, and global capitalism shape people's lived experiences without privileging the study either of discourse or of capitalist relations of production.

The conditions under study in this book are often the subjects of research in the field of international development. In the years following World War II, development was generally associated with economic growth and the accumulation of physical capital in the Third World. Since the 1980s, there has been a greater emphasis on human capital and on "creating agents who can become more productive through their acquisition of knowledge, better health and nutrition, and increased skills" (Meier, 2001, p. 19). In either case, development remains synonymous with the growth of the economy even though this may not translate into greater political freedom at the societal level (Sen, 1999) or into a reduction in individuals' sense of vulnerability to forces they cannot control (Markee, 1997). These alternative definitions of development—as greater freedom or as a reduction in vulnerability—are important when exploring the meaning of *maisha magumu* because the phrase describes not only the absence of good health and employment but also the desire for more control over broader social and political-economic forces.

Since the early 1990s, another strand of research on development has emerged that has influenced my own. In these anthropological studies, the institutional structures and the discursive strategies of development become the objects of investigation (Escobar, 1995; Ferguson, 1994, 1999; Gupta, 1998;

Jennings, 2001; Kelsall & Mercer, 2002; Pigg, 1992, 1997; Rothenberg, 2001). In some cases, the researchers foreground the structural apparatus itself to explore how development institutions operate (cf. Ferguson, Kelsall & Mercer); in others, they emphasize the discourse used by development planners and the tangible effects it has on program development and on program participants' sense of self (cf. Pigg, Rothenberg). A common assumption in these studies, and in my own, is that "there cannot be a materialist analysis which is not, at the same time, a discursive analysis" (Escobar, 1996, p. 46). Indeed, one of my goals in this book is to encourage scholars, policymakers, and activists to reconsider theoretical boundaries between 'the material' and 'the discursive' in order to interrogate the conventional wisdom—one might even say wishful thinking—that schooling is sufficient to transform social and political-economic relations around the world.

One of the dominant themes in development discourses from the colonial period to the present is *education as panacea*. I use this phrase to describe the enduring faith that schooling will effect profound social change in the Third World, even in places where political-economic conditions make such transformations highly unlikely. Other scholars have described similar phenomena, as in Stambach's phrase "schools-to-the-rescue models" (2000, p. 11) and Tyack and Cuban's notion of school reform as "tinkering toward utopia" (1995, p. 1). Recently, I heard the phrase "education as a panacea" at a conference even though the presenters had not read this manuscript.[7] The theme that connects these studies and my own is the disjuncture between, on the one hand, pronouncements about schooling and, on the other, policies about development that do little to ameliorate poverty for the long term. As Tyack and Cuban put it, "Producing sonorous rhetoric about solving social problems through education is easier than carrying out fundamental social change through schooling" (1995, p. 61). One would be hard pressed to find a better example of this point than the international development discourses about girls' education and development discussed in the next chapter.

The Desire for Schooling and the Role of the Imagination

The chapter to follow looks at several dominant themes in contemporary international development policy to help us understand policymakers' positive attitudes toward women's education. However, the analysis of policy discourse does not explain the desire for schooling among individuals who are often not privy to documents produced at meetings in Rio, Cairo, or Washington, D.C. One of the differences between this study of schooling and the ones cited in the paragraph above is my interest in how the *education–as–panacea* concept acquires meaning at the local level. How, for instance, does one make sense of the sacrifices many parents make to pay for their children's schooling when they know very well that good jobs do not await the majority of graduates? Approaches other than those used for policy analysis are necessary to answer this and similar questions about people's aspirations and actions at the local level.

Appadurai's (1996) work on the imagination and Boym's (2001) study of nostalgia are useful in exploring the question of why people in Old Moshi are enamored of schooling even though it may result in neither formal employment nor in an alleviation of *maisha magumu*—or it may even, as William's story illustrates, worsen the condition.[8] Although Appadurai and Boym do not work in Tanzania, their projects are relevant nonetheless. For instance, they both draw attention to the ways that temporal and spatial relations have been redefined by migration and 'virtual' migration through television, film, and the Internet. Many more people now imagine themselves or their children migrating and migrating to places familiar to them through images from the mass media or from migrants who leave and return with greater ease than in the past. They note the importance of the collective, or the 'imagined community,' that these images help to create (c.f., Anderson, 1983). Appadurai, for example, makes a distinction between fantasy—a private, temporary longing—and imagination, which he sees as a collective, future-oriented vision. He writes that imagination "creates ideas of neighborhood and nationhood, of moral economies and unjust rule, of higher wages and foreign labor prospects" (1996, p. 7). Similarly, Boym defines nostalgia in collective terms: It is "about the relationship between individual biography and the biography of groups or nations, between personal and collective memory" (2001, p. xvi). Although Boym uses nostalgia to mean visions of the past and of the future, I restrict its use to instances of retrospection by people in Old Moshi even though I concur with her that a longing for the past can have a profound impact on the future.

How do Appadurai and Boym's insights on the imagination and nostalgia, respectively, contribute to an exploration of the desire for schooling in postcolonial Tanzania? First, we find that migration affects the very definition of a good parent in Old Moshi. Today, as in the recent past, parents strive to send their children to school because they recognize that fewer and fewer youth will be able to make a living on the overpopulated mountain. Many parents hope that secondary schooling will provide the knowledge and the credentials necessary for employment elsewhere in the country (see Chapter 3). Migration is also a central feature of Tanzanian youth discourses about schooling, with the English word "sponsor" punctuating conversations in Swahili about finding someone who can pay for an aspiring student to study abroad. More and more young people have friends or family members living beyond Tanzania's borders, and many of the youth I have come to know over the past decade imagine themselves living in these other places, too (Vavrus, 2002b).

The idea of a collective vision of the future and of the past is also relevant for my argument about *education as panacea*. I contend that it is the desire for schooling—and not primarily the content of the formal curriculum—that is driving down the fertility rate in the Kilimanjaro Region (Chapter 3) and driving up the risk of HIV/AIDS among young women who cannot afford a postsecondary education but who nonetheless want it very much (Chapter 4). Secondary school graduates imagine themselves as members of a collective transnational class of 'educated persons,' and they strive to demonstrate their status in many ways, including having small families they can care for properly under the conditions of *maisha magumu* (Levinson & Holland, 1996). Fertility rates are declining in the region even though there is no sex education in most schools; it seems likely, then, that the higher education-lower fertility correlation in Kilimanjaro is the result of factors that are not present in the school curriculum.

In addition to these examples, the economic problems facing coffee farmers today, as prices approach their nadir, create a sense of nostalgia for certain institutions from the past. The furrow societies that regulated irrigation on Mount Kilimanjaro are examples of these. As discussed in Chapter 5, the plan to resurrect these nearly defunct societies suggests that individuals are concerned about their ability to keep earning a livelihood from the land, but they are expressing this concern through "a collective memory, a longing for continuity in a fragmented world" (Boym, 2001, p. xiv).

Thinking about nostalgia and imagination in these ways leads me to believe that the desire for schooling in Old Moshi is not merely the result of global cultural homogeneity as more children attend Western-style schools. The postcolonial condition is far too complex to distill the forces responsible for social change down to the school system alone. I suggest, instead, that educational desire in this case is derived from many factors, including the more than 100 years of missionary schooling in the community, the more frequent encounters with international development agencies and agendas, and the search for security at a time when global capitalism heightens feelings of insecurity. In sum, these are the dimensions of the postcolonial condition most salient to contemporary life in this particular locale.

Background to the Study

Mapping Old Moshi

My relationship with Old Moshi began in 1992, when I accompanied a fellow researcher on a visit to Njema Secondary School.[9] I was in Tanzania at the time because my husband, Tim, was spending the year conducting research for his dissertation. We had met in Tanzania two years earlier during a Swahili language program, and I decided to defer my doctoral studies for a year to assist with his research and to improve my Swahili. After several months, it became clear that his project was unfeasible. We struggled with this problem and concluded that it would be best to find something else to do with the remainder of our time in Tanzania. We then contacted the ELCT to see whether any of their schools needed short-term instructors. Njema was selected for us because I could fill in for an absent Form 2 English teacher, and Tim could teach mathematics to the Form 3 students. With little further ado, we commenced a relationship that continues to the present.

From our prior research, we knew that the Kilimanjaro Region was privileged in many ways. Although the region constitutes only 5% of the total population, it hosts 9% of the students enrolled in public secondary schools and 21% of the students attending private secondary schools (MOEC, 1996; see also Table 3 in Chapter 2). Moreover, Kilimanjaro has the lowest percentage of women and men with no formal education of any region in the country (Bureau of Statistics Tanzania and Macro International Inc., 1997), and one of the country's highest primary school enrollment rates (MOEC, 1996). In terms of health services, Kilimanjaro has approximately 9% of the country's hospitals and dispensaries and the largest percentage of children who have been vaccinated: a striking 94% compared to the national average of 71% (Bureau of Statistics Tanzania and Macro International Inc., 1997). It is also noteworthy that the region is undergoing an incipient fertility decline, with the total fertility rate decreasing from

Map 2: Moshi Municipality, Old Moshi, and the General Location of the Schools in This Study

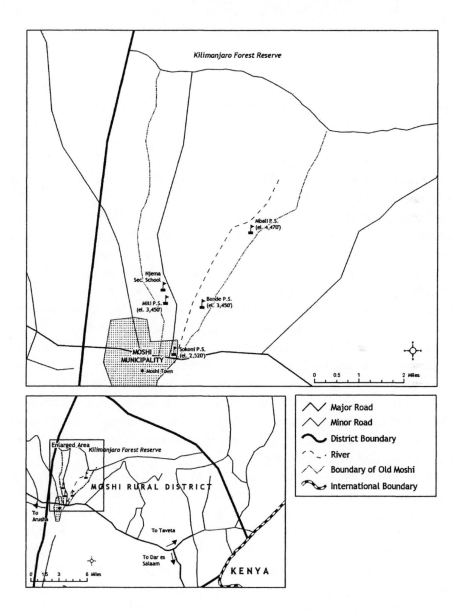

7.0 in 1973 to 5.4 by the late 1980s (Larsen, 1996). Fertility in Tanzania as a whole has also declined in recent decades—from 6.6 in the late 1960s to 5.8 by the mid-1990s—but the decline in Kilimanjaro is particularly noteworthy because it is coupled with a low mean ideal number of children and with high rates of modern contraception (Bureau of Statistics Tanzania and Macro Inter national Inc., 1997; Larsen, 1996; Richey, 2001). Thus, women in Kilimanjaro generally want smaller families than women elsewhere in the country, and they are more likely to use modern contraceptives to achieve this goal.

Unbeknownst to us at the time, we were about to move to a former chiefdom—Old Moshi—with many historical advantages because of its prime geopolitical location on the slopes of Mount Kilimanjaro (see Chapter 2). Like other areas on the mountain, Old Moshi is organized vertically because of the deep north-south valleys carved by rivers flowing from glacial springs near the mountaintop. Its elevation ranges from approximately 2,500 feet at the base of the mountain to 4,500 in the north. The northern boundary of Old Moshi is marked by the lush Kilimanjaro National Forest Reserve, through which tourists pass to ascend the Kibo and Mawenzi peaks of the mountain. The eastern boundary is the Nanga River, and the Msaranga River forms the western boundary. The southern edge of Old Moshi is identified by one of the major transportation routes in Tanzania: the tarmac road that connects the coastal cities of Tanga and Dar es Salaam to the northern cities of Moshi and Arusha. There are no paved roads in Old Moshi, but there is one dirt road running north to south that is passable during the rainy season, and there are several smaller north-south roads that are often unusable during this season from March through May. The steep escarpments have prevented the building of east-west roads; however, there are numerous well-worn footpaths that cross the riverbeds and ascend the valley walls.

Today, Old Moshi has approximately 20,000 inhabitants living in some 2,500 households (Bureau of Statistics, 1990; Moshi, 1994). It is divided into the Old Moshi East and Kimochi wards, and each one is further subdivided into four villages. Each village has at least one primary school (with 11 in total), and seven of the eight villages are connected to the national electricity network. All of the villages have access to water at public standpipes, but they vary considerably in the percentage of households with piped water (see Chapter 5). Most of the adults in the eight villages are farmers whose families have ½ to 3 acres of *kihamba* land upon which they grow their stable food, bananas, and the major cash crop, Arabica coffee. Many families also own several acres of land on the plains that lie south of the tarmac road, where they grow maize and, occasionally, sunflowers (Moshi, 1994).

In addition to farming, adults and youth are often engaged in other forms of labor, including teaching, masonry, mechanics, carpentry, and clerical work in the town of Moshi, approximately 6 miles away. Women, in particular, are frequently involved in selling produce, clothing, and sundries at one of the two small markets in Old Moshi or at the large market near the tarmac road. The generational and gender differences in economic activity in Old Moshi are similar to the ones described by Setel in his study of Mbokomu, the former chiefdom lying due west of Old Moshi (1999). Setel found that only one-third of the farmers were under the age of 30, while approximately 80% of the petty traders and the unemployed were in this age group. In the Moshi Rural District, where both Mbokomu and Old Moshi are located, Setel discovered that women made up more than half of the 15–54-year-old population. This, he suggests, means that men are more likely to migrate from rural communities on the mountain to urban areas like Moshi, Arusha, and other towns in Tanzania.

Regardless of age or sex, the vast majority of Old Moshi residents identify themselves as Chagga and as Lutheran. With 95% of the population fitting into both of these two categories, the community appears rather homogeneous at first glance (Moshi, 1994). However, there are important social and economic differences between the villages in the Old Moshi East Ward on the western side of the Msangachi Valley and those in the Kimochi Ward on the eastern side. As we will see in Chapter 5, a much greater percentage of families in Miti and Sokoni villages (Old Moshi East Ward) have electricity and piped water in their homes compared to the families in Bonde and Mbali villages in the Kimochi Ward. Furthermore, many more Standard 7 students from Miti and Sokoni Primary Schools started Form I in 2001 than did their counterparts across the valley.

The differences between villages in Old Moshi are primarily geopolitical. Miti, for instance, is the village nearest the former chief's residence, where much political activity took place before and during the German and British colonial periods. In the 1920s, the British established a Central School in Miti, one of only six such schools in the entire country where select young men could obtain an education beyond Standard 4 (*Report*, 1926). In the 1970s, the school was turned over to the YMCA and became the private secondary school known today as Njema. It continues to be the educational center of Old Moshi, and the people of Miti village benefit greatly from their proximity to it.

The villages of Miti and Sokoni have the further advantage of being located along the only road in Old Moshi that is passable throughout the year. Because the road is in relatively good condition, secondary school-age youth living in Sokoni can make the trip to Njema with much greater ease than young people who live across the steep valley in Bonde or Mbali villages. Moreover, Sokoni village lies along the tarmac road leading to Moshi and to its good public secondary schools. The youths' proximity to this urban center is an important advantage for them because students who pass the national Primary School Leaving Examination at the end of Standard 7 generally prefer to attend the cheaper and often better public secondary schools in town. Living near a town like Moshi is also advantageous for students whose families can afford 'tuition' classes after school, on the weekends, and during school holidays. Many children from Sokoni and Miti go into town to attend these classes during the long mid-year holiday in June, giving them a further advantage over the youths in Bonde and Mbali who live farther away and whose families generally have less money to spend on schooling. In sum, there are clear ethnic and religious similarities among the residents of Old Moshi, but there are also important historical, political, and economic differences as explored in the following chapters.

Mapping the Methodological Terrain

In 1993, the quotidian responsibilities of teaching at Njema kept me quite occupied and left little time for the formulation of the dissertation topic I promised to produce during the year in Tanzania. Yet my participation in school events and the "open-endedness" of conversations unencumbered by a research agenda were far more educative than I realized until I was back in graduate school in Wisconsin (Peterson, 2000, p. 50). The experience of living in Miti and teaching at Njema served as the filter through which I poured my readings on economic development, international education, and feminist theory. Those that helped me make sense of my observations in Old Moshi were reworked and rearticulated in my dissertation proposal, the blueprint for an ethnographic study of schooling and declining fertility in the Kilimanjaro Region. Some of the theoretical readings that most influenced my research include Bourdieu and Wacquant (1992), Escobar (1995), Ferguson (1994), Foucault (1980), Fraser and Gordon (1994), Greenhalgh (1995), Mohanty (1991), and Popkewitz (1993).

Returning to Old Moshi in 1996 filled with abstract ideas about discursive power, subjectivities, and regimes of truth, I spent the first few weeks simply getting used to changes in the discourse: First, there was the switch from English to Swahili as the dominant medium of conversation except in the classroom, and second, there was the striking difference in conversational topics and tropes. For instance, I found myself engaged in discussions with students, colleagues, and neighbors about topics seldom broached in my academic community in the U.S., such as the importance of becoming a 'born again' Christian in this dangerous era of AIDS or the painful struggle to cope with declining incomes and rising costs as captured in the phrase *maisha magumu*. These conversations did not negate the relevance of the social theories I brought along with me; they simply confirmed the sentiments of my fellow graduate student, who believed that a university education often kept Africans and Africanists like ourselves "[o]ne step removed from the nitty-gritty of a situation" (Peterson, 2000, p. 225).

The re-adjustment process was facilitated by scaling back my formal research plans during the early months to make time for visits with neighbors and friends who wanted to see our 8-month-old son, August. His presence sparked many lively discussions about the topics of schooling and family planning, which provided ideas about questions to ask during formal interviews later in the year. After several months of teaching and 'hanging out' with neighbors, I felt ready to embark on the more formal aspects of the research project. With the assistance of two secondary school graduates, Sarah Kwayu and Aklei Kessy, we conducted one-on-one and focus group interviews with female and male students at Njema. Ms. Kwayu and I also interviewed young women living in Old Moshi who had completed primary school but had not continued to the secondary level (Vavrus, 2002a). In addition, I interviewed teachers, school officials, and community leaders involved with education in Old Moshi and in the Kilimanjaro Region as a whole.

Although participant observation and interviewing were the primary methods of data collection, I also engaged in survey and archival research. Charles Moshi helped me design and conduct a survey of adults in three villages in Old Moshi, two in the Old Moshi East ward and one in the Kimochi ward. The survey, conducted at the midpoint in the fieldwork year, provided numerous insights into the emerging theme of *maisha magumu* and its relationship to schooling and fertility decline. We also designed and administered a written survey to students at Njema and at another secondary school in Kilimanjaro to get information about their parents' level of education, their family's material resources, and their goals for the year 2000. In addition, the students were asked to write short essays about some of the themes that had emerged from interviews, including *maisha magumu*, corporal punishment, and differences in the 'moral character' of girls who do and do not attend secondary school. I also asked these students to write down their home address if they wanted to continue with this research project in four years if I were to return to Old Moshi in 2000 as I hoped to do.

The archival research for the project took place in Dar es Salaam during the six-week holiday in June and July. At the National Archives, I gathered information on British colonial education policies; at the main government hospital, Muhimbili, I read through dissertations pertaining to schooling and adolescent health; and at the offices of the Ministry of Education and Culture, the World Bank, the Canadian Embassy, and several non-governmental organizations (NGOs), I spoke with officials about my project and collected documents on girls' education. These multiple methods generated much of the material discussed in Chapters 2 through 5.

In the summer of 2000, I began a new research project in Old Moshi as part of a postdoctoral program in anthropological demography. This study consisted of two parts: a written survey of Standard 6 and 7 students at Bonde, Mbali, Miti, and Sokoni primary schools, and a survey/interview with the students' parents or guardians. The students' survey asked about their class rank, their academic and employment aspirations, and their reproductive health behavior. It also contained questions designed to assess the students' literacy and numeracy skills. The comprehensive survey/interview for the adults sought to ascertain the family's educational history, the mother's birth history, the parents' socioeconomic status, and their aspirations for the child in the study. In total, there were 277 child-adult pairs from the four villages in the study. Chapter 5 presents an analysis of some of the data from the surveys of both children and adults.

The trip to Old Moshi in 2000 also presented the opportunity to contact the students from 1996 who had indicated their interest in continuing with the research project. Thus, I mailed a survey to 225 young women and men who had completed the survey four years earlier, when they were in secondary school. There were fewer people in the 2000 study than in the 1996 one because some students had not consented to being a part of future research, and a few others had given me the address of their secondary school rather than a home address where they could be contacted in the future. The follow-up survey touched on many topics, including the level of schooling completed since 1996, current employment status, marital status, use of family planning, and attitudes about economic changes in the country that had occurred over the past four years. There was also an essay question that asked the participants to write about significant events that had occurred in their lives since 1996. They were not given specific topics about which to write, but schooling, health, and *maisha magumu* were clearly the most prominent themes in their essays. Fifty-six percent of the questionnaires and essays (125 out of 225) were returned to me, and I have included 112 of them in the analysis presented in Chapter 4 because they contained both a completed questionnaire and essay.[10] The essays were translated from Swahili into English by a Tanzanian Swahili instructor, and the major and minor themes were then coded independently by my research assistant and me.

In the summer of 2001, I returned to Old Moshi to carry out two follow-up projects: one related to the mail-in survey described above and the other based on the 2000 survey of primary school students and their parent/guardians. With the help of Zaina Mshana, a recent secondary school graduate, we contacted the students still living in Kilimanjaro who had returned the mail-in survey and invited them to attend one of four focus group discussions to talk about the results of the survey. Chapter 4 describes the discussions we had about the theme of HIV/AIDS, and I have written elsewhere about the topic of educational language policy that also came up in several of the meetings (Vavrus, 2002b).

The second follow-up project conducted in 2001 was another survey of the adults interviewed in 2000 and focus group discussions with them to talk about the findings from the previous year's survey. The primary objective of the follow-up survey was to find out which children who had been in Standard 7 in 2000 had begun secondary school at either a public or private institution in 2001. Rather than try to locate all of the children from the 2000 survey—some of whom were far away at boarding school or living with distant relatives—we designed the follow-up survey for the adults because we knew the location of their homes. The 2001 survey asked specific questions about the secondary or technical school the child was now attending as well as about the child's current activities if she or he was not in school. The follow-up survey also asked questions about topics mentioned in the open-ended sections of the 2000 survey that were not part of the formal questions. In particular, I had not included detailed questions about people's sources of water and agricultural activity in the 2000 survey, but it became clear to Mr. Moshi and me that we ought to ask about these topics in the follow-up survey because parents were clearly linking them to schooling.

To learn more about parents' views on the relationship among schooling, agriculture, and water, we invited them to attend focus group discussions at Bonde, Mbali, Miti, and Sokoni primary schools. Mr. Moshi and I held seven discussions—two at each school with the exception of one at Sokoni—in which we talked about the cost and quality of schooling in the community, the problems parents face as coffee farmers unable to make a decent living off the land, and the possibility of water shortages if the predicted disappearance of the ice cap on the top of Mount Kilimanjaro proves correct. Discussions about the present condition of *maisha magumu* often turned to nostalgic comparisons with "the past," when schooling was inexpensive, coffee prices were high, and water was regulated through clan-based furrow societies. The most animated points in discussions came in response to our question about parents' support for a proposed cost-sharing arrangement in the water sector, whereby Old Moshi residents would be charged a fee for piped water at public and private taps as a means to promote water conservation. The strong negative reactions to this privatization program reflected, in part, the conviction that such a plan would intensify *maisha magumu* for poor families; however, the participants' responses also indicated the profoundly symbolic value of water in a community where relationships based on clan affiliation are still quite strong (see Chapter 5).

The final stage of the research discussed in this book took place in 2002, when Mr. Moshi and I went back to the four primary schools to report on the findings from the 2000 and 2001 surveys and from the focus group discussions. After our presentation at each school, we asked the assembled parents, teachers, and community leaders to help us interpret the data. During the same trip, I interviewed members of several NGOs in the Kilimanjaro Region working on the problems identified by people in Old Moshi during the course of this longitudinal study, namely, the problems of youth unemployment after primary school, HIV/AIDS, and environmental degradation. These interviews are discussed in the final chapter, where I consider the achievements and the limitations of NGOs for long-term development in Tanzania.

During the six years covered in this book (1996–2002), I have used many different research methods and spoken with myriad individuals about the desire for schooling amid conditions of real or perceived decline (see Table 2). I have also explored with young and old the meaning of development and the role that schooling plays in its realization. In the end, I am struck by the power of nostalgia and of the imagination to reshape the past, affect the present, and propel the future. Nostalgia for the furrow societies, for instance, has more to do with the future than with the past, more to do with people's anxieties about their livelihoods than with a genuine desire to resurrect the 1930s. The past and the future, both of them colored by the imagination, combine to form the present. In Appadurai's words, "The imagination is today a staging ground for action, and not only for escape" (1996, p. 7). Thus, the desire for schooling and the life of an 'educated person' is not the mere expression of an oftentimes unrealistic goal; it also becomes the engine for action. In some cases, the action is counter-productive because it can put young women at greater risk of contracting HIV/AIDS by having sex with men who pay for the girls' schooling in return (see Chapter 4); in other instances, the desire for schooling for one's children may bring community members together to oppose policies likely to compound the effects of economic decline (see Chapter 5). Action and imagination are integral to the *education-as-panacea* concept as we will see in the chapters that follow.

Table 2: Summary of the Research Process

Dates	Methods	Primary Participants
1996	Participant observation	Secondary school students and teachers
	Interviewing (one-on-one and focus groups)	Secondary school students and teachers, education officials, female primary school leavers
	Survey interviewing	40 adults in Old Moshi
	Survey (written)	282 students at Njema and at another secondary school in the Kilimanjaro Region
	Archival research	Tanzania National Archives, the Ministry of Education and Culture, and other official offices
2000	Survey (written)	277 Standard 6 and 7 students

Continued on next page

Table 2 (continued)

Dates	Methods	Primary Participants
	Survey interviewing	277 parents/guardians of the Standard 6 and 7 students
	Mail-in survey	225 former secondary school students from the 1996 study
2001	Survey interviewing (follow-up)	Parents/guardians of the Standard 7 students from the 2000 study
	Focus group discussion	7 meetings with parents/guardians at Bonde, Mbali, Miti, and Sokoni Primary Schools
	Focus group discussion	4 meetings with former secondary school students from the 1996 study who completed the mail-in questionnaire in 2000
	Observation	Projects of two Tanzanian NGOs: Mkombozi Vocational Training Centre and the Qoheleth Foundation
2002	Presentation/discussion	4 meetings with parents/guardians, teachers, and village officials to discuss the results of the 2000–2001 surveys
	Interviewing (one-on-one and focus groups)	Members of four Tanzanian NGOs: KIWAKKUKI (Old Moshi branches), Mkombozi Vocational Training Centre, Qoheleth Foundation, and the Tanzanian Environmental Action Project (Mbokomu branch)

Summary of Chapters

The next chapter presents an overview of the major theoretical perspectives on schooling to show how these views have affected the study of women and development since the 1970s. I then explore representations of women's schooling as a panacea in contemporary development texts. Taking examples of policies produced at United Nations conferences and by the World Bank, I show how influential development institutions conceptualize schooling for women as a solution to development dilemmas in the Third World. The trope of the "feminist modern" is one of several discursive strategies I examine in relation to the *education–as–panacea* concept (Greene, 1999, p. 227). Although the educated, empowered feminist modern is the antithesis of the oppressed Third World women of earlier development policies, I argue that this more recent figure still does not signal the transformation of social and political-economic relations that are necessary for long-term development. In fact, because 'she' seems to be doing so well on her own, the feminist modern is a distraction from these larger, harder transformations.

In Chapter 2, the focus shifts and tightens, from international policy to local practice, where the contemporary issues of population, HIV/AIDS, and environmental conservation reveal the historical processes that have shaped them. Working chronologically, I consider changes in social policy, with an emphasis on schooling, during the 20th century. This was a period of numerous social and political-economic transitions, as Tanzania changed hands from German to British colonial rule and then went from a socialist to a neoliberal state during the postcolonial era from 1961 to the present.

Chapter 3 begins the ethnography of the present, exploring the possible contributions of schooling to fertility decline as widely noted in international population and development discourses. A portrait of life at Njema Secondary School illustrates the complexity of the education-fertility relationship; there students confront *anti*-family planning messages and construct their own pro- and anti-abortion positions based on notions of Christian morality and biomedical knowledge. The chapter also highlights some of the challenges in producing culturally-sensitive reproductive health curricula, as advocated in international policy, because of local disagreements over what constitutes Chagga culture and how cultural norms about large families are changing in response to *maisha magumu*.

Chapter 4 builds on the preceding ones in exploring the relationship among schooling, HIV/AIDS, and economic hardship in northern Tanzania. It revisits the students described in Chapter 3, who participated in follow-up studies in 2000 and 2001 that were designed to map the changes in these young people's lives after they completed secondary school. The chapter opens with excerpts from focus group discussions with some of these graduates that show how sexual risk, condom *disuse* in particular, is born of economic necessity—and a degree of bravado—for young people in northern Tanzania. These views are then situated within the literature on AIDS and structural adjustment in Africa that lends support to many young people's contention that the desire for schooling in an era of economic decline contributes to sexual risk-taking, even among relatively well-educated secondary school graduates like themselves. Their secondary-school experience appears to have whetted their appetite for higher education, even if paying for it means young women frequently have unprotected sex with the "sponsors" of their schooling.

Chapter 5 contributes an additional perspective on the development dilemmas facing the residents of Old Moshi by showing how recent changes in water and agriculture policies in Tanzania affect parents' ability to send their children to school. Using the example of a proposed water privatization program for the Kilimanjaro Region, I argue that parental support for schooling in this community cannot be studied in isolation from the political-economic relations that constrain people's ability to make a living off the land. Once again, we see that the *education–as–panacea* concept does not fully capture the impact of economic decline on people's ability to support schooling in their community.

In the final chapter, I pull together the main ideas of the preceding ones by looking at four Tanzanian NGOs that address the interconnected development problems of schooling, unemployment, HIV/AIDS, and environmental degradation. The interviews with leaders of local NGOs and the descriptions of their groups' activities shed light on the ways local organizations situate the specific material concerns of their community in broader national and international discourses and movements. On the one hand, development discourses shape the way NGO leaders see themselves—for example, as agents of empowerment—but on the other hand, there are distinct local circumstances to which these community leaders remain attentive. These compelling examples of Tanzanian organizations that combine education and economic activities provide the basis for the recommendations in the concluding section, which address the specific conditions in Old Moshi without being limited to one locale.

NOTES

1. The names of the villages, schools, and informants in this book are pseudonyms. However, I have opted to identify Old Moshi as the site of the study because the history of this chiefdom-cum-administrative district is essential to the analysis of the contemporary local situation. With permission, I have also used the real names of several people who assisted with the research project, including Mr. Charles Moshi, whose contribution to this study is immeasurable. In addition, the names of the individuals and organizations discussed in Chapter 6 are real because they requested I cite them in this way.

2. All of the interviews were conducted in Swahili unless noted. Whenever a word was uttered in English, it is indicated in italics.

3. The model for this table comes from Sharp's book on secondary schooling in Madagascar (2002). Her study provides a very compelling example of postcolonial education in Africa.

4. I use the term *Third World* in this book while remaining conscious that it is frequently a synonym for 'underdeveloped.' The term was first employed by representatives at the 1955 Bandung Conference in Indonesia to express their countries' non-alignment with capitalist or socialist world powers. Robert Young suggests using *Third World* "as a positive term of radical critique even if it also necessarily signals its negative sense of economic dependency and exploitation" (1990, p. 12). It is in this sense that I use the term whenever it is necessary to draw attention to enduring geopolitical inequalities in 'Southern' or 'developing' countries.

5. Although the terms *education* and *schooling* are often used interchangeably, I believe it is important to distinguish between them. Cremin (1978) gives a comprehensive definition of education:

> Education [is the] deliberate, systematic, and sustained effort to transmit, evoke, or acquire knowledge, attitudes, values, skills, or sensibilities, and any learning that results from the effort, direct or indirect, intended or unintended. This definition obviously projects inquiry beyond the schools and colleges to a host of individuals and institutions that educate—parents, peers, siblings, and friends, as well as families, churches, synagogues, libraries, museums, settlement houses, and factories. And it clearly focuses attention on the relationships among the several educative institutions and on the effects of one institution's efforts on those of another. (p. 701)

Schooling more narrowly describes efforts to transmit knowledge and attitudes in one particular institution—the school. Although *education* is used frequently in this book, it should be borne in mind that my primary concern is with idea of formal knowledge transmission in schools.

6. Pennycook (1998) and Gandhi (1998) make a further distinction between postcoloniality and postcolonialism, but I have chosen to place both of these concepts under the rubric of the postcolonial condition. Postcoloniality is sometimes differentiated from postcolonialism, with the former drawing attention to the lasting impact of the "economic deprivations of colonialism" and the latter to the cultural and ideological aspects of colonialism that continue to influence the present (Pennycook, 1998, p. 39). From my perspective, postcolonial theory loses its pertinence for contemporary Tanzania if it does not help one to analyze both the ideological and the economic legacies of colonialism.

7. My thanks to Carolyn Kissane for drawing my attention to the Tyack and Cuban reference and to Hanne Mogensen for introducing me to Anne Katahoire and Susan Reynolds Whyte, the two panelists at the Annual Meeting of the African Studies Association who discussed the *education-as-panacea* concept in their presentation about reproductive health in Uganda (December 7, 2002).

8. My thanks to Tom Popkewitz for introducing me to Boym's work.

9. I owe a debt of gratitude to Amy Stambach for hosting me in Kilimanjaro and for sharing her enthusiasm for educational research in Tanzania.

10. The response rate for this study is not as high as the 75% figure that some organizations set as their minimum rate (Fowler, 1993). However, the lack of verifiable addresses for many participants and the movement of young people around the country make the 56% rate an acceptable figure for my purposes. In fact, when I discussed my plan to conduct a mail survey in Tanzania with a noted survey researcher at Harvard, he told me that there was no precedent for such a study, so he recommended I attempt it to see whether even half of the surveys were returned (T. Mangione, March 2000, personal communication).

Chapter 1

International Development and the Feminist Modern

If education were a panacea, then we could address the general problems facing many African nations—AIDS, environmental degradation, and others—by solving the problems that beset the education system: poor teacher training, lack of facilities, limited access. Yet welcome as these interventions would be in Tanzania and elsewhere, they cannot be understood without situating them within the broader context of international development. The privileged place of schooling, especially for women, in post-World War II development discourses is inextricably linked to visions of modernization and economic expansion in the Third World. In this chapter, I discuss three perspectives on schooling—functionalism, neo-Marxism, and postmodernism—in relation to the topic of women/gender and development.[1] These perspectives are marked by certain distinguishing features, but there is also considerable overlap between them in some cases. I have chosen to examine them chronologically to reflect the period when each one became prominent in international development discourses, but this does not mean that the emergence of one led to the demise of the others. On the contrary, these perspectives co-exist, though not necessarily in the same spheres; neoliberalism tends to have more influence in international financial institutions, neo-Marxism and postmodernism in the academy. I then use aspects of neo-Marxist and postmodern theory to analyze policy documents from several international conferences held during the past decade, documents that illustrate the current neoliberal consensus about women's schooling and development.[2] I am particularly interested in the emergence of the "feminist modern" figure in development discourses of the past decade because it represents a further entrenchment of the *education-as-panacea* idea (Greene, 1999, p. 227).

Women's Schooling and National Development

In keeping with broad forces of western social thought, largely inherited from the twin thrusts of the Reformation and the Enlightenment, we place education among the highest of the various agencies supportive of change and progress for societies, economies, and individuals. For more than two centuries we have maintained, rather uncritically, this faith in the influence of education.

—Harvey Graff, 1979

The Functionalist Perspective

Some of the most enduring beliefs about women's schooling and national development in the Third World are derived from functionalist theories of modernization. Functionalism dominated American social science research from the late 1950s to the early 1970s, and its legacy is still evident in discourses stressing the importance of 'human capital' for national development. Based on biological models of the relationship between parts of the body to the whole, functionalism assumes that institutions interact in a similar way to maintain the entire social system (Peet, 1999; So, 1990). Schools play a particularly important role in system maintenance because it is here that young people learn solidarity with their social group as well as the specialized roles and skills needed by that group (Feinberg & Soltis, 1998).

Functionalism serves as the foundation for modernization theories that seek to explain how societies move from 'traditional' to 'modern' stages of development. From a functionalist perspective, modernization is a total social experience, one that affects the political, economic, and cultural spheres of life. Proponents argue that modernization reconfigures "urbanization, industrialization, secularization, democratization, education, [and] media participation" in concert to promote the shift from tradition to modernity among individuals and their societies (Lerner, 1958, cited in Huntington, 1968, p. 32; Rostow, 1960). There is a psychological dimension of modernization as well, and here schools play an especially crucial role, inculcating the values of a modern person: education itself, science and technology, civic and international concern, flexibility and change, and personal responsibility (Inkeles & Smith, 1974; Inkeles, 1998). Moreover, schools help to produce the putatively critical 'need for achievement' and entrepreneurship that make the modern person productive in a market economy (Adelman, 2001; McClelland, 1961).

A functionalist notion of modernization undergirds human capital theory, still the most widespread explanation today as to how schooling affects national development. As Shultz puts it, "Thus, in a nutshell, the persistent increase in the demand for the high-quality services of human agents is a function of the additions to the stock of useful knowledge. The complexities of the additions to this knowledge have been much greater in recent, modern economic growth than during early, relatively simple industrialization" (1998, p. 40). Human capital theory contends that if societies are ever going to move from 'the traditional' to 'the modern,' then the population must have the requisite skills and knowledge—human capital—to participate in the new economic environment. Therefore, national economic growth depends largely on the education and health of the labor force and not simply on a nation's physical capital, such as its roads and factories (Meier, 2001). Moreover, human capital theory suggests that schooling promotes economic and social development because it produces positive externalities, or 'spillover effects,' that benefit the community and the nation rather than only the individual student. For instance, positive social benefits from investments in female human capital development include improvements in maternal health, in child care, and in domestic sanitation (Cleland & van Ginneken, 1988; Jejeebhoy, 1995; Kabeer, 1994; LeVine et al., 1991).

The need to improve women's access to schooling in order to promote national development propelled the Women in Development (WID) movement of the 1970s and early 1980s. Women in Development advocates argued that without proper training for employment in the modern economy, women would be excluded from modernization, and national development would therefore suffer (Boserup, 1970; Rogers, 1980). Schooling for women would help create gender equity in the labor market and a more efficient social system as women learned, and then applied, the same modern skills that men were learning. The WID view did not challenge the basic tenets of modernization theory, such as its embrace of capitalism, its evolutionary view of social change, and its economic rationale for women's schooling; instead, WID advocacy drew attention to gender stereotypes and prejudices in development policy and practice that prevented women from reaping the fruits of development that modernization is thought to produce (Kabeer, 1994).

The Neo-Marxist Perspective

The WID perspective faced increasing criticism in the 1980s as neo-Marxist feminists called for broader transformations of the international development agenda.[3] In contrast to functionalism, neo-Marxism contends that it is conflict between social groups rather than consensus among them that is the normal state of political-economic affairs. As might be expected, the two perspectives differ on the role of schooling, with functionalists suggesting that it promotes social cohesion and development and neo-Marxists arguing that it reproduces gender, race, and class-based inequalities (Feinberg & Soltis, 1998). From the latter perspective, schools are implicated in the production of ideologies that legitimate the status quo and in the reproduction of these inequalities through the cultivation of cultural capital for some groups but not for others (Bourdieu, 1977; 1984; Bowles & Gintis, 1976).

Shifting to the specific topic of women's schooling and development, neo-Marxist theories seek to explain how the structures of capitalism and patriarchy work in combination to doubly disadvantage women in the Third World (Beneria & Sen, 1981; Fernandez-Kelly, 1983; Ong, 1987; Stromquist, 1992, 1998). Dependency theory, for example, contends that global capitalism functions through collusion between the elites of the periphery—the Third World—and those of the core—the First World; together, they further their own interests at the expense of the majority (Amin, 1982; Cardoso & Faletto, 1979; Frank, 1967). The inequalities identified at the international and national levels also operate at the household level, where women's undervalued domestic labor is linked to the demands of capitalism and to the patriarchal household relations it requires (Kabeer, 1994).

The neo-Marxist perspective also highlights the unequal modes of production between periphery countries, which export raw materials, and core countries that process and consume most of these goods. The role of the state, neo-Marxists argue, should be to protect 'infant industries' in the Third World from competition in international markets (McMichael, 1996). The Woman and Development movement (WAD) presents a parallel platform of female development that attempts to protect women from the detrimental effects of patriarchy through projects created by and for women alone (Parpart & Marchand, 1995). For example, WAD advocates hope that women's cooperatives, by excluding men, will foster female solidarity and reduce patriarchal control over relations of production. However, the WAD movement has been criticized by some feminists, especially organizations from the Third World that object to its view of women as independent from their productive and reproductive relations with men (Kabeer, 1994).

The Postmodern Perspective

Postmodernism presents a third perspective from which to view women's schooling and national development. To review for a moment, the functionalist notion of modernization is most concerned with the human and physical resources that Third World countries need if they are to "take off" from their traditional stage of development and reach a modern (capitalist) stage (Rostow, 1960). In contrast, neo-Marxism uses a dialectical model of development in which conflicting interests among social groups are inevitable but may nevertheless eventually produce synthesis in the form of social equality. While there is an affinity between certain strands of neo-Marxism and postmodernism, the latter emphasizes discourse as a form of power through which social reality is constructed. Additionally, postmodernism is defined by its skepticism toward metanarratives, or grand theories, used to explain the operations of social and political-economic forces. In other words, postmodernism raises questions about the very existence of a universal 'thing' like patriarchy and orients research toward an examination of the discursive relations that shape people's taken-for-granted assumptions about the world.

The postmodern influence in development studies is apparent in research examining the ways power operates through the production of recurring images about the Third World. For instance, some scholars have looked at dominant motifs in the mass media about women in Africa, Asia, and Latin America. Others have considered the bureaucratic structures of development institutions themselves in an effort to understand how the institutions produce the discourses through which people express their commonsense views about the 'real' Third World (Lutz & Collins, 1993; Mohanty, 1991; Pigg, 1992, 1997; Spivak, 1999).

Located in the interstices between WID and WAD is Gender and Development (GAD). With its focus on the socially-constructed categories of masculinity and femininity rather than on biological differences between men and women, GAD appeals to critics of the economic orientation of WID and to skeptics of the broad claims about patriarchy and capitalism offered by WAD.

A GAD approach to improving girls' achievement at school, for example, would examine the specific social and political-economic factors in a community that produce gendered patterns of school enrollment and performance; it would not assume *a priori* that girls are out of school because of 'traditional' stereotypes (the WID approach) or patriarchal domestic arrangements that are inevitably produced by capitalist modes of production (the WAD approach). GAD presents an important framework for feminist analysis of schooling and development by considering how gender relations are constituted in different contexts, but it, too, has its critics.

Although the emphasis on discursive power does not preclude political engagement with programs seeking to combat material inequalities, there is considerable debate between some neo-Marxists and postmodernists over the very possibility of a postmodern feminism. Critics of postmodernism argue that feminist politics becomes impossible if one does not claim an affiliation with women as a coherent group in the struggle against patriarchal oppression (Hartsock, 1990). In addition, if postmodernism disavows grand theory, so the argument goes, then it cannot engage seriously in women's struggles against global capitalism. However, I believe there is much 'real' political ground to be gained through discursive analysis because the categories and assumptions inscribed in texts manifest themselves in material ways in women's and men's lives. For instance, we can consider the insights from Mohanty's analysis of representation in development discourses:

> This average third world woman leads an essentially truncated life based on her feminine gender (read: sexually constrained) and her being 'third world' (read: ignorant, poor, uneducated, tradition-bound, domestic, family-oriented, victimized, etc.). This, I suggest, is in contrast to the (implicit) self-representation of Western women as educated, as modern, as having control over their own bodies and sexualities, and the freedom to make their own decisions. (1991, p. 56)

Without examining the recurring images and assumptions about the targets of development interventions, one cannot understand how the postcolonial condition is comprised by the discursive *and* the material legacies of colonialism, developmentalism, and global capitalism. Thus, I concur with Fraser and Gordon that it is possible—even desirable—to combine the analysis of discourse with political engagement to ameliorate the social and political-economic conditions that negatively affect women's (and men's) lives in different contexts (1994).

In the next section, I focus on the place of women's schooling in contemporary developmentalism by analyzing several important international policies of the past decade. This examination is essential to understanding the *education-as-panacea* concept and the reasons why schooling for women figures prominently in development programs designed to combat such varied problems as overpopulation, HIV/AIDS, and environmental degradation.

Development 'Crises' and Conferences

> Women and girls play a particular role in these 'redemptive' [policy] declarations. Out of all the groups who have suffered in the twentieth century, their experiences are drawn upon and identified in such reports. On one level, this is a welcome development for feminists, who have long criticised the absence of any international recognition of the educational demands of girls and women. On the other hand, the special significance given to women by such diverse bodies as the World Bank and small NGOs (non-governmental organisations) raises questions about such a consensus.
> —Elaine Unterhalter, 2000

The international consensus that schooling for women is central to national development is a relatively recent phenomenon. Although the WID movement drew attention to women's role in the modernization process, it is only during the past decade that women's schooling has become "[p]erhaps *the* cause célèbre of education and development" (Sutton, 2001, p. 78; emphasis in original). A review of research on schooling in Africa, for example, found that in the late 1980s few studies focused on women, but that this had changed dramatically by the early 1990s, when almost all of the 240 projects reviewed discussed women and girls' formal education (Samoff, 1999).

One can't help but wonder why the change in policy priorities. One reason is certainly the shift in prevailing opinions within the field of development economics: from the 1950s and 1960s, when an interventionist state was considered critical to the modernization of the Third World; to the 1970s and 1980s, when neoliberalism championed a small state and free markets as the key to development; to the mid-1990s and into the present, when neoliberals advocate public-private partnerships for basic social services to improve economic growth (Vines, 2001).

Neoliberalism has become a catchall term in development and in "anti-development" discourses in recent years (Elyachar, 2002, p. 495), but I use it to describe specifically the articulation of a set of political policies, neoclassical economics principles, and human capital theory. The pro-privatization and decentralization policies of the Reagan and Thatcher governments in the 1980s illustrate the "evil government view" common to most neoliberal political administrations (Adelman, 2001, p. 113). The Reagan-Thatcher opposition to state regulation, for instance, complemented neoclassical economic theory that had gained prominence in international development discourses by this time. Neoclassical economics contends that open markets with minimal government interference will lead to national economic growth. According to Meier, "correct [i.e., neoliberal] policies were to move from inward-looking strategies toward liberalization of the foreign trade regime and export promotion; to submit to stabilization programs; to privatize state-owned enterprises; and to follow the dictates of the market" (2001, p. 19). Meier explains that along with this reduced role for the state in orchestrating development came a move away from physical capital investments (roads, bridges, schools, hospitals) and toward human capital development. From a neoliberal perspective, economic growth does not come from state planning but from the knowledge and skills of "forward-looking, profit-maximizing agents" (Romer, 1986, cited in Meier, 2001, p. 19).

Neoliberalism, in its political and economic forms, has had a profound effect on development policies in the Third World because the leading international financial institutions—the International Monetary Fund (IMF) and the World Bank—have generally embraced it (Adelman, 2001). For instance, during the global economic crisis of the 1980s, the Bank issued special loans to poor countries to support broad structural adjustment programs (SAPs), but the loans required approval from the IMF. The IMF's strict anti-inflationary policies called for sharp reductions in state spending on social services, such as health care and schooling. To compensate for this loss of government funding, the populations of many poor countries have been brought into so-called cost sharing, or cost recovery, programs—in other words, they pay fees for services that were previously free or almost free (Turshen, 1999). As Stiglitz argues, IMF conditions on structural adjustment loans may have reduced government expenditures, but they have also made education both more important and much more expensive. He notes that "families in many developing countries, having to pay for their children's education under so-called cost recovery programs, make the painful choice not to send their daughters to school" (2002, p. 20). The gendered dimensions of SAPs in Tanzania, and the painful choices they demand, are discussed in Chapter 4.

In the past decade or so, the World Bank has moved away from a full embrace of 'small-state' neoliberalism. Instead, it now generally supports public-private collaboration in which the state plays a somewhat larger role in the provision of services that enhance human capital development, i.e., that improve the basic education and health of the population. However, the market remains free from government regulation, and individuals pay steep fees for post-primary schooling because the social rates of return are considered lower at these levels (Todaro, 1989).

The small-state philosophy that has dominated international development for the past few decades provides a rationale for promoting women's schooling of a particular type in the Third World. Jones (1997) argues that the Bank began a "crusade" in the 1970s, urging borrowing countries to make public investment in primary schooling and to impose user fees at the secondary and tertiary levels (1997, p. 122). Bank economists emphasized as well the importance of equity and decentralization, because these would improve the quality and the efficiency of the school system. Taking Jones's analysis a step further, we can see that women's schooling became an ideal target for development interventions because it tapped into equity and decentralization concerns without calling into question the social and economic disparities compounded by structural adjustment policies. Because only a modest gender gap at the primary level exists in most regions of the world today (the exceptions are South Asia and some Arab states), socioeconomic disparities rather than gender disparities could have become *the* cause championed by international development institutions (Knodel, 2003). However, they have not, and gender differences remain at the top of the development priority list.

Along with the issue of gender equity, the promotion of decentralization through community empowerment and management helped to focus attention on women as pivotal local stakeholders and as potential entrepreneurs (Elyachar, 2002). These decentralization discourses were circulating through development institutions at the same time that feminist researchers and activists were making significant inroads in international policy circles. In particular, the articulation of decentralization with women's schooling was facilitated by the formation of the "triple roles framework" in the 1980s, which drew attention to the multiple demands on many women as mothers, wage earners, and community managers (Moser, 1989). The framework contained a critique of development agencies that treated women "as cheap labour for a variety of interventions" (Kabeer, 1994, p. 276); however, its focus on the local, i.e., the household and the community, also had the effect of essentializing women's *roles* and, therefore, of insufficiently analyzing gender *relations*.

Neoliberalism and WID/GAD feminisms have helped reshape international policy over the past decade to create a new visibility for women's schooling in many different areas of development. These new priorities were evident as early as the 1990 World Conference on Education for All held in Jomtien, Thailand, where schooling for women was declared a top priority for international development agencies. The consensus that emerged from the Jomtien conference constituted a shift in the very meaning of basic education, because it was, for the first time, linked to words such as *women, empowerment,* the *environment,* and *population*: "Indeed, it is no exaggeration to say that Jomtien marked the emergence of an international consensus that education is the single most vital element in combating poverty, empowering women, promoting human rights and democracy, protecting the environment and controlling population growth" (UNICEF, 1999, p. 13).

In the years since Jomtien, a number of international conferences have strengthened this consensus about the power of women's schooling to solve, or very nearly, the big problems of Third World countries. And despite the closing of the gender gap in education in most regions of the world, the 'crisis' in international education has been defined primarily in terms of women's lack of access to schooling. Policymakers and activists are rightly concerned about barriers to female enrollment and achievement wherever they exist, but the narrow focus on gender discrimination obscures other political-economic crises that deeply affect women's lives.

My use of the term *crisis*, both here and elsewhere in the book, is based upon Stuart Hall et al.'s *Policing the Crisis* (1978). In it, Hall and his co-authors suggest that crises are produced, not simply discovered, and they examine the complex process by which popular and scholarly attention comes to be focused on certain problems and not on others. Their example is the panic about black youth and violence that swept Britain after several highly publicized muggings. Shock and outrage escalated into a full-blown crisis in public opinion, even though, as the authors show, the number of attacks, and therefore their general importance, was actually quite small. This leads them to consider how the media represented these events in relation to other racial and economic tensions in the country.

Applying these insights to my research, I contend that gender-based discrimination is a serious problem that keeps girls out of school in many places. Nevertheless, economic and political crises triggered by certain neoliberal policies have not received the attention they deserve, in part because doing so would call into question the "cookie-cutter approach" to structural adjustment formulated by international financial institutions (Adelman, 2001, p. 118). For many politicians and policymakers, it is more comfortable to target cultural stereotypes about gender than it is to address the political economy of international development in which they themselves may be implicated.

We can begin to consider the ways that crises are policed by examining the problems and solutions identified in several international development policies. The 1992 United Nations Conference on Environment and Development (UNCED) held in Rio and the 1994 International Conference on Population and Development (ICPD) that took place in Cairo provide ample material for such an investigation,[4] as does a World Bank report entitled *Education and HIV/AIDS: A Window of Hope* (2002). Taking the UNCED, ICPD, and World Bank documents as typical examples of international development discourses, I look at how they represent the role of women's schooling in combating disparate development problems. In particular, I am interested in the categories and assumptions that hold these texts together as a body of discourse and give it the authority to turn discursive representation into action. To conduct such an analysis, I turn to the seminal work in postcolonial studies by Edward Said.

In *Orientalism*, Said explains his method for studying the discursive construction of the Orient (1978). The task, he writes, is to understand "the sheer knitted-together strength of Orientalist discourse, its very close ties to the enabling socio-economic and political institutions, and its redoubtable durability" (1978, p. 6). To accomplish this formidable undertaking, Said uses a method he calls "strategic formation" to study the connections among texts and between texts and society (p. 20).[5] He does this by looking at stylistic features of Orientalist narratives and the socio-historical context in which they were written to demonstrate that these texts are representations and not descriptions of reality. Substituting 'developmentalism' for 'Orientalism,' I adopt a similar strategy in order to examine the discursive devices in development policies that produce the very problems women's schooling is supposed to solve.

There are many connections among the UNCED, ICPD, and World Bank documents that merit discussion, but I limit my comments to the themes that are most germane to the analysis in the subsequent chapters, namely, culture, human capital, and women's empowerment. Beginning with the concept of culture, the documents reveal a tension surrounding schooling and social change that emerged during the colonial period and lingers into the present. As I will discuss in Chapter 2, colonial education and health policies in Tanzania vacillated between a view of African culture as the cure for political-economic crises in the colony, and African culture as the very cause of these problems (Colwell, 2001). In contemporary development discourses, one also observes this tension between embracing 'indigenous knowledge' and local customs on the one hand, and blaming 'traditional' attitudes and values on the other. For example, the UNCED document states repeatedly that education about child spacing (p. 28), family size (p. 42), and reproductive health services (p. 47) should be "in keeping with freedom, dignity and personally held values and taking into account ethical and cultural considerations." The ICPD policy is more specific about how to incorporate cultural considerations into population and health education so long as they do not compromise the accuracy of the scientific knowledge conveyed: "Information, education and communication activities should rely on up-to-date research findings to determine information needs and the most effective culturally acceptable ways of reaching intended audiences" (p. 60). If materials about reproductive health and HIV/AIDS are not already in existence in the schools, then the ICPD suggests that "education projects should be based on the findings of sociocultural studies and should involve the active participation of parents and families, women, youth, the elderly and community leaders" (p. 61).[6]

These two documents, especially the policy from the ICPD, recognize the importance of cultural dimensions of reproductive health and the different cultural contexts in which population and health education occur. This is a welcome change from the population discourses of the 1970s and 1980s, when family planning took precedence over reproductive health and women's rights (Greene, 1999). However, policies that adhere to a culture-as-cure perspective are based on the functionalist assumption that "society is underpinned by a value consensus and that the various institutions in society contribute to the ongoing stability of the whole" (Taylor et al., 1997, p. 24). In other words, these policies suggest that young women, elderly men, and community leaders share a set of cultural precepts by virtue of living in the same society and that these shared values will lead to a consensus about how to teach reproductive health in the schools. The ethnographic description of Njema Secondary School in Chapter 3 illustrates the difficulty in implementing culturally acceptable teaching about population and health issues when people's views of 'their' culture are so varied.

The culture-as-cause perspective presents an even more simplified view of culture because it divorces the cultural dimensions of population and health from the political-economic ones. For instance, the World Bank's policy on education and AIDS begins with a section entitled "How We Got Here" (p. 3). Only one of the seven items discussed mentions political-economic factors by name (in reference to commercial sex); moreover, it is assumed throughout the document that the Bank's macroeconomic reform program—SAPs—will alleviate rather than exacerbate the spread of the disease. Instead of considering its own culpability, the World Bank presents the primary obstacles to AIDS prevention as cultural, not political-economic. For instance, phrases like "extended family networks," "cultural and religious conservatism," and "denial of the problem" by local and national officials in the Third World focus attention on culture as *the* cause of the spread of HIV/AIDS rather than as one factor among several (p. 3). When disease is constructed primarily as a cultural problem, schooling becomes a logical solution because it is assumed that a lack of modern scientific knowledge leads people to engage in high-risk sex. The World Bank document suggests, for example, that schools by their very definition "have the benefit of staff equipped with the tools of teaching and learning," and that they are normally places "where adolescents can obtain accurate information on reproductive health" (p. 30). These statements reflect the idealized view of schools as sites where up-to-date knowledge is conveyed, but we will see in Chapters 3 and 4 that accurate *and* inaccurate reproductive health information circulates in them. Furthermore, the ethnographic research described in the following chapters shows that the desire for ever more schooling may contribute to high-risk sexual behavior among youth who have "accurate information" about AIDS but choose not to put it into practice.

In addition to the theme of culture, a second organizing concept in the UNCED, ICPD, and World Bank policies is human capital development. More specifically, these influential documents assert again and again that the enhancement of women's human capital is the *sine qua non* of national development. References to human capital theory abound as the texts explain why educational programs for women will ameliorate the problems of high fertility, AIDS, and environmental degradation. Although education and health—the twin pillars of human capital development—are critical for women *and* men, developmentalism links them primarily to women and to the state's need for cost-effective development. The Bank document, in particular, makes many arguments about the cost-effectiveness of women's formal education for human capital development:

> •Girls' education can go far in slowing and reversing the spread of HIV by contributing to female economic independence, delayed marriage, family planning, and work outside the home. (p. xvii)

> •It [schooling] is highly cost-effective as a prevention mechanism, because the school system brings together students, teachers, parents, and the community, and preventing AIDS through education avoids the major AIDS-related costs of health care and additional educational supply. (ibid.)

> •Secondary school education is what really makes a difference to increasing age at marriage, delaying first sexual encounters, improving negotiation for protected sex, and promoting other risk-reducing behaviours. Ensuring girls' access to secondary school is also key to better employment opportunities for women, and often an opportunity to break the cycle of poverty and reduce the risk of exposure to HIV. (p. 47)

Women's human capital development is also discursively linked to cost-effective national development strategies in the UNCED and ICPD policies, but these documents situate the discussion within broader discourses of poverty alleviation and female empowerment than does the World Bank text.[7] For instance, the UNCED document identifies education and women's rights as an "effective strategy" for dealing with environment and development problems. It continues with its four primary objectives of sustainable development and poverty alleviation, one of which is to "create a focus in national development plans and budgets on investment in human capital, with special policies and programmes directed at rural areas, the urban poor, women and children" (p. 27). The ICPD document reinforces this articulation of sustainable development with human capital development, explaining the critical contributions of women's education to population reduction and national development: "Education is a key factor in sustainable development....The reduction of fertility, morbidity and mortality rates, the empowerment of women, the improvement in the quality of the working population and the promotion of genuine democracy are largely assisted by progress in education" (p. 57). The ICPD text, like the UNCED one, places education—women's education, in particular—at the center of "population-environment relationships" because of the positive effect education is assumed to have on the protection of natural resources (p. 60). This recognition of women's role in population change and environmental conservation is a positive change from the era when women were not visible in development discourses, but there is also the problem of placing unrealistic demands on women to promote national development.

Culture and human capital development are inextricably related to the third recurring theme in these policies, namely, women's empowerment. My position is one of strong support for efforts to increase women's control over their productive and reproductive lives and to reduce their vulnerability to political and economic forces. However, the discourses of empowerment illustrated by these documents construct, to varying degrees, a highly autonomous female subject upon whom much of the responsibility for national development falls. Consider the following examples:

> •Empowerment of women is essential and should be assured through education, training and policies to accord and improve women's rights and access to assets....Population/environment programs must enable women to mobilize themselves to alleviate their burden and improve their capacity to participate in and benefit from socio-economic development. (UNCED, p. 39)

> •These events [other UN conferences] are expected to highlight further the call of the 1994 Conference for greater investment in people, and for a new action agenda for the empowerment of women to ensure their full participation at all levels in the social, economic and political lives of their communities. (ICPD, p. 6)

> •Girls' education can go far in slowing and reversing the spread of HIV by contributing to poverty reduction, gender equality, female empowerment, and awareness of human rights. It also has crucial implications for female economic independence, delayed marriage, family planning, and work outside the home. (World Bank, p. 7)

The repetition of key phrases—"empowerment," "mobilize themselves," and "economic independence"—illustrates the process Said described as strategic formation, whereby a body of discourse becomes authoritative through intertexual references to the same phenomenon (1978, p. 20). In this case, the authority of developmentalism to mobilize policy about women in the Third World is derived, in part, from a common vocabulary about formal education leading inevitably to female empowerment.

Education as Panacea and the Feminist Modern

In contrast to the oppressed Third World woman described by Mohanty (1991), the female figure who has emerged in development discourses since the early 1990s can be described as "the feminist modern" (Greene, 1999, p. 226). This woman is granted far more agency to change her own circumstances than was her counterpart in population discourses from the 1960s to the 1980s. According to Greene, "Thus, what marks the feminist modern as modern is the emphasis on women as subjects capable of performing on their own, or with the help of experts, particular techniques to improve their health and welfare" (1999, p. 227). Greene appropriately notes the importance of supporting efforts to make women subjects, rather than objects, of development policies. However, he also challenges us to think about the complexity of modernity and the ways that we "conceptualize ourselves as subjects capable of transforming ourselves as particular objects for improvement" (ibid.). In other words, developmentalism conceptualizes women in the Third World as capable of transforming themselves, but it presupposes a particular kind of improved person with 'modern' beliefs, attitudes, and behaviors.

If we consider Greene's notion of the feminist modern in relation to the UNCED, ICPD, and World Bank documents, what would it reveal about the themes of culture, human capital, and empowerment? First, the feminist modern emphasizes the problem noted above, namely, that culturalist arguments tend to downplay the role of political-economic forces in shaping development dilemmas. A recent statement on women's education by the Executive Director of the United Nations Population Fund, Nafis Sadik, exemplifies this tendency:

> There are many obstacles to closing the continuing gender gap in education, but none of them are insurmountable. Many of these are solely in the mind....Poverty is frequently offered as a reason for marrying off young girls, but I think a far more powerful motive is the cultural conservatism that assigns no value to girls except as future wives and mothers. A girl's future is often predetermined and her choices and options pre-empted by cultural norms and practices. Culture that denies choice to women must be changed. (cited in UNESCO, 2000, p. 18)

This construction of the problem leaves little room for disagreement because, certainly, conservative views do curtail women's education and health options under certain circumstances. However, Greene reminds us that when patriarchal culture becomes the primary target of development interventions, it diverts attention away from "countercausalities"—political and economic forces—that also have a profound effect on women's lives (1999, p. 224).

The feminist modern further reveals the influence of neoliberalism on the field of international development during the past 15 years. For instance, the language of cost-benefit analysis is widely used to justify women's schooling and health programs; therefore, it has now become common sense to discuss policy-making as a neutral, technical matter rather than as a conflictive political process where different groups vie for representation. As we will see in Chapter 5, cost-benefit analysis in the arena of environmental policy downplays the politics of social service provision and the struggle between the state and its citizens to pay for these services.

Third, the feminist modern draws attention to the trope of empowerment that has become in recent years one of the most important taken-for-granted assumptions in development. An empowered woman is one who takes an active role in controlling her fertility, practicing safe sex, and protecting the environment, and schooling is supposed to help her achieve these goals. Despite the desirability of such a scenario, however, women's choices about childbearing, reproductive health, and environmental conservation are shaped by social and political-economic considerations that the independent figure of the feminist modern does not take into account. We will see in the chapters to follow that there are numerous limitations on schooling to provide accurate sex education or to empower young women to make wise decisions about their reproductive health.

Conclusions

The discursive shift from the "always oppressed" Third World woman Mohanty critiqued to the female figure cogently described by Greene illustrates one of the most important transformations of international development policy in the post-war era. It certainly shows that feminists—liberal, neo-Marxist, and postmodern—can effect institutional change and policy reform at the highest levels. However, one must ask whether the greater agency afforded to the feminist modern in these documents will lead to the transformation of social and political-economic relations necessary for international development efforts to be sustained. My view is that we ought to be cautious about calling every neoliberal policy "democratic" simply because it promotes a "shift to the people and away from the developmentalist state" (Elyachar, 2002, p. 510). The co-optation by international financial institutions of potentially democratic development practices, such as community members' involvement in developing health education programs, raises questions about whether these moves usher in a more equitable post-development era or whether they simply relocate the onus of development from Third World states to Third World women. In particular, does the current embrace of local knowledge and culture inevitably lead to democratic participation in development, or is this turn to the local "a new type of discipline that circumvents the state" (Elyachar, 2002, p. 511)?

Another reason for doubting the democratic potential of the feminist modern stems from its emphasis on women as individual targets for development interventions rather than on gender relations as the site for social transformation. I contend that developmentalism has made *women* visible without a concomitant re-visioning of the macroeconomic environment that shapes *gender relations*. The narrow focus on the individual in these texts lifts the burden for development from international financial institutions and national policy makers and places it squarely on communities and individuals, especially on women. At first glance, discourses of decentralization appear empowering for women because the potential is there for greater control by female actors of economic and political decision making. This may, indeed, be the case in some situations. However, reconfiguring public (state)/private (community or individual) relationships will not necessarily bring about democratic transformations in gender relations without concomitant changes in the national and international political-economic climate.[8] Before considering such changes in Chapter 6, we move back in time in the next chapter to see how the discourses of the present resound with representations of the past.

NOTES

1. The term *paradigm* could have been used instead of the more pedestrian "perspective" that I have opted for in this book. An excellent study of the major paradigms in educational research is Popkewitz (1984). In it, he defines *paradigm* as follows:

    > The idea of paradigm directs attention to science as having constellations of commitments, questions, methods and procedures that underlie and give direction to scientific work. The importance of paradigmatic elements in science is that they do not appear as such but form the 'rules of the game' or dispositions that guide everyday practice....As people are trained in a research community, they learn ways in which to think, 'see', 'feel', and act toward the world. These dispositions towards the world are implicit in the exemplars of a field that the researcher learns as s/he defines the scope and boundary of inquiry. (p. 33)

    These important considerations of commitments, dispositions, and discourses are central to the discussion of perspectives in this chapter.

2. There are many definitions of policy, with most of them based on "rational models" that assume consensus among different social institutions (a functionalist model) and linear stages from conception to implementation to evaluation (an evolutionary model) (Taylor et al., 1997, pp. 24–25). In contrast, my notion of policy is derived from a sociocultural approach that emphasizes process, power, and practice (Ball, 1994; Levinson & Sutton, 2001; Shore & Wright, 1997). This approach suggests that policy is a statement of an institution's stance on an issue, but that every stance is a political strategy designed to effect change in a particular direction. Additionally, a sociocultural approach to policy analysis is concerned with practice, or "what is enacted as well as what is intended" (Ball, 1994, p. 10).

3. There are a number of differences between orthodox Marxism and neo-Marxism. The three most important reasons for my focus on neo-Marxism in this study are, first, its attention to gender, race, *and* class relations in the formation of inequality; second, its view of cultural production in social institutions, such as schools and the media, as central to the analysis of capitalism; and third, its greater specificity about how inequality is produced, maintained, and contested in different contexts (Feinberg & Soltis, 1998).

4. The UNCED document I examined is entitled *Agenda 21: Programme of Action for Sustainable Development* (United Nations, 1994). It conveys the final set of agreements negotiated among the governments at UNCED. The ICPD document is entitled *Population and Development: Programme of Action adopted at the International Conference on Population and Development*, Cairo, 5–13 September 1994 (United Nations, 1995).

5. The other method of discursive analysis used by Said is "strategic location," which means locating an author in relation to the entire corpus of Orientalist literature (1978, p. 20). It is this process that most clearly distinguishes Said's method of analysis from Foucault's archaeological approach, to which Said repeatedly notes his debt. Whereas Foucault questions

the importance of determining authorship of texts, Said believes that the durability of Orientalism derives from authors' referencing of one another's representations. The issue of authorship is not central to my analysis because the UNCED, ICPD, and World Bank texts were written by committees and not by individuals. However, I do note occasions where one of these texts references another because, as Said, I believe this cross-referencing process helps create the "knitted-together strength" of influential discourses (1978, p. 6).

6.   One of the most serious shortcomings of international policy about education is the almost complete absence of critical reflection on the production of knowledge through the formal and informal curriculum. Apple's extensive writings on this topic draw attention to the myriad social functions of the curriculum, especially those that reinforce inequalities based on race, class, and gender (1982, 1990, 1993). If a more complex understanding of the conflicts surrounding the production and implementation of curricula were infused in policy, then one would hope to find such complexity reflected in the materials eventually developed for classroom use in different contexts.

7.   Unterhalter (2000) provides a useful discussion of the distinctions among several other important education and development policies produced in the 1990s: the 1990 Education for All conference in Jomtien, Thailand, the 1995 Beijing World Conference on Women, and the World Bank's 1995 *Priorities and Strategies for Education*. The ICPD, like the Beijing conference, pays far more attention to poverty alleviation as a precursor to women's empowerment than either the UNCED or the World Bank texts. Although I am looking at discursive similarities in the ICPD, UNCED, and World Bank documents, there are also subtle yet significant differences among them that warrant further study.

8.   The analysis in this chapter has benefited greatly from a rereading of Popkewitz (2000) and from my discussions with him and his students at the University of Wisconsin-Madison. Although I was unable to incorporate all of their suggestions here, I have attempted to develop several of them in Vavrus (forthcoming).

Chapter 2

Transformations in Schooling in Northern Tanzania

> If we had transcended colonial images and narratives more comprehensively, perhaps we would not need to discuss them at all—but there is no emptiness at present in which such a confident silence can be heard.
>
> —Nicholas Thomas, 1994

The international population, health, and environment policies discussed in the previous chapter illustrate the central place of schooling in contemporary development discourses. However, the *education-as-panacea* concept did not appear on the world stage without historical antecedents. During the colonial era, schooling was used in different parts of Africa to draw converts to Christianity and to produce 'modern' citizens with favorable dispositions toward colonial social and political-economic policies. After World War II, the belief that formal education—modeled after schools in the United States and Europe—would promote modernization and discourage socialism provided the rationale for bilateral and multilateral development assistance during the decades of decolonialization (McMichael, 1996). During the 1960s and 1970s, when Tanzania and a number of other African countries put into place socialist development programs, schooling once again had pride of place in discourses about creating social transformation.

In this chapter, I consider the factors that have transformed the social and physical landscape of Old Moshi from the late 19th century to the present. In contrast to the chapters that follow, I rely here on primary and secondary documents rather than on ethnographic observations and interviews. I begin the chapter by looking at narratives written by Europeans who encountered the famous Chief Rindi of Old Moshi during their travels to Mount Kilimanjaro before colonial rule was established. I move then to the German and British periods to examine colonial administrators' and missionaries' perspectives on schooling. The final section of the chapter covers the shifts in Tanzanian development policy since independence that have affected people's lives on the mountain, especially the change from the socialist orientation of President Julius Nyerere to the neoliberal development model that has gained ascendancy during the past two decades.

Old Moshi Prior to World War One

Comparatively safe and well fed in the leafy fastness of their beloved Kilimanjaro, the Chagga have always looked down on the flat, hot, arid land below from a position of geographical advantage. Their climate, their soil, their water have favored them. In most years they have good rainfall. And water also comes from streams that flow from the high forest belt, some of it descending dramatically in rushing brooks over great boulders, dropping in waterfalls into roaring pools. Tamed water too quietly moves for miles in winding narrow irrigation canals the Chagga have dug for centuries to moisten their richly productive, well manured banana groves.

—Sally Falk Moore, 1986

The relative prosperity of Old Moshi compared to the rest of rural Tanzania is due, in part, to rainfall, irrigation canals, and rich volcanic soil that enhance agricultural production on Mount Kilimanjaro (Moore, 1986). The first European travelers to reach the mountain noted some of these features of the landscape, but they were especially enchanted by the snow at the summit of the mountain. For instance, J. L. Rebmann, a German missionary, visited the area three times and sent back to Europe in 1848 the first reports of "the lofty mountain Kilimanjaro, capped with eternal snow" ("Invitation," 1878, p. 448). Other missionaries and explorers followed Rebmann and verified his reports of snow on an equatorial mountain in Africa. Several of them, including Charles New and Hans Meyer, retraced Rebmann's trip to Old Moshi and wrote about the environment on the mountain as well as their encounters with Chief Rindi, perhaps the most famous Chagga chief of the 19th century. New's book, entitled *Life, Wanderings, and Labours in Eastern Africa*, described his journey in 1871 from the coast along the Indian Ocean to "Moche" (Old Moshi) and eventually to the snowline of Kilimanjaro. In addition to describing the vegetation and sketching the mercurial Rindi, New noted his wonder at the Chagga irrigation system: "The water-courses traverse the sides of the hills everywhere; and now I understood what I had been told upon the coast, viz., that the Wachagga make the water in their country to run up hill!" (1873 [1970], p. 370). Meyer, who in 1887 became the first European to reach the summit of Mount Kilimanjaro, also wrote about the sophisticated irrigation canals on the mountain and concluded that resolving irrigation canal disputes were "the weightiest duties" for Chagga chiefs (1891, p. 103).

Chief Rindi, born around 1845, had many weighty duties, not the least of which was forging political alliances with neighboring Chagga clans to consolidate the Old Moshi chiefdom (Stahl, 1964). The tales by foreigners suggest that Rindi was "the acknowledged master of the [diplomatic] games being played with Europeans from...1862 until the late 1880's" (Rogers, 1972, p. 107). Because of his precarious position between the powerful chiefdoms of Kibosho in the west and Marangu in the east, Rindi wanted to establish a solid relationship with the Europeans, whose power often surpassed that of his Chagga rivals (Smith, in New, 1873 [1970]). In 1885, representatives of the British Church Missionary Society (CMS) visited Old Moshi, and Rindi gave them land to begin the first school for children in the area (Shann, 1956). The chief's agreements with missionaries to establish schools, clinics, and churches provided important political and economic advantages for the people of Old Moshi: "[T]hough its area and population remained small, the [Old] Moshi folk got a head-start over those of other Chagga chiefdoms in receiving the newly introduced benefits which, from the Chagga point of view, could all be turned to practical, and sometimes political advantage" (Stahl, 1964, p. 257).

The early advantages that accrued to the people of Old Moshi did not last long after Rindi's death in 1891, which was also the year that formal German rule began on the mountain. The chief's son, Meli, became chief after his brother, the rightful heir to the chiefdom, was murdered (Stahl, 1964). Meli and his rival, Chief Marealle I of Marangu, used the presence of competing mission societies and competing German administrators in their two chiefdoms to try and bring about the downfall of the other. With the Lutherans in Old Moshi aiding Meli and the Roman Catholics providing support to Marealle in Marangu, the chiefs had greater military resources to use against each other (Rogers, 1972). The conflict grew until Chief Marealle, in 1900, convinced the German captain at the military base in Marangu that Chief Meli and the chief of Kibosho were plotting against the German administration. The two chiefs were tried and hanged in Old Moshi, as residents of the community looked on (Stahl, 1964).

The German presence in Old Moshi continued to grow in the 1890s after colonial administrators built a large base—or *boma*—on land that belonged to Chief Rindi. The German Leipzig Lutheran missionaries also became active in the community, establishing a mission station near the *boma* (Rogers, 1972).

During these early years of mission schooling, many Chagga parents were skeptical of the benefits that might accrue to them by sending their sons—daughters did not attend—to school. Some parents, in fact, wanted to be paid by the missions for the labor lost when their sons were in school. However, the importance of having a child who could read and write grew as encounters with Europeans increased, so new schools for boys and even a few for girls were quickly established in Old Moshi during the first decade of the 20th century.

There is limited information about the curriculum at mission schools during this period—and schooling was almost exclusively a mission activity until after World War I—but it appears that most schools emphasized the training of catechists to benefit the church rather than the preparation of clerks who might benefit the German administration.[1] First and foremost, the Leipzig Lutherans sought converts who could be trained as teachers and evangelists to work in communities on the mountain. Mission schools emphasized lessons about the Bible, but they gradually expanded the curriculum to include basic literacy and numeracy skills, music, hygiene instruction, and geography (Lema, 1968).

While the number of converts to Christianity remained low until after World War I, both the Lutheran and Catholic churches were making inroads in Kilimanjaro through the schools affiliated with their mission stations. By 1910, after some 25 years of missionary activity on the mountain, it was estimated that 4% of the population was Christian, with approximately 1,300 Lutherans and 3,000 Catholics out of a total of approximately 100,000 people in Kilimanjaro (Maro, 1974). The fruits of these early evangelical plantings can be seen today: 95% of the population of Old Moshi is Lutheran (Moshi, 1994).

It was during the German colonial period that coffee farming began on the mountain, an activity that along with schooling would lead to significant economic and social changes in Kilimanjaro in the decades to come. Introduced by European settlers and missionaries in the 1890s (Coulson, 1982), coffee seedlings grew well in the middle-altitude belt on the mountain and provided a way for some Chagga to pay hut taxes to the German administration rather than engage in forced labor (Howard & Millard, 1997).

While private ownership of land has a long history among the Chagga, there were specific rules about its distribution and use that changed with the introduction of coffee. In brief, Chagga chiefdoms were made up of clans, and each one had rights over a parcel of land that it considered sacred because of the ancestors buried there. A grave, explained Rogers, "was considered proof that the land of that area belonged to the clans whose ancestors were buried there, and such an area of settlement and sacred association strongly resisted the inter-ference of chiefs or anyone else" (1972, p. 39). Alongside the communal owner-ship of land by the clan was the important system of inherited land rights for first and last-born sons, a system that continues today to govern the establish-ment of *vihamba* (*kihamba*, singular)—the ancestral garden and burial grounds found across the mountain (Rogers, 1972; Setel, 1999).

The profits from growing coffee waxed and waned depending on interna-tional markets, but by the beginning of World War I, there were a number of Chagga men involved in coffee production. There was also a group of men and a smaller group of women who had gone through mission schools and were reaping some of the benefits of their education, earning a salary either by teach-ing in mission schools or by working for the German colonial administration. The importance of these two developments—coffee farming and schooling—were only beginning to be understood during the pre-war period, but they took on increased significance during the British colonial era and in the decades fol-lowing independence.

The British Era in Kilimanjaro

Although information about schooling during the German colonial period is rather limited, this is not the case for the interwar years of British colonial rule in Tanganyika. During the years between the wars, the number of mission, gov-ernment, and Chagga-run schools expanded in Kilimanjaro but so, too, did ten-sions over the role of schooling in preserving 'tradition' while also promoting social change. Many Lutheran missionaries held that schooling was disrupting traditional Chagga culture, and, for a time, British government administrators also developed "tribal schools" for the preservation of certain cultural practices (Mumford, 1929, 1930). Colonial education policy, however, soon moved in the other direction, toward "adaptation," in the hope of hastening social and eco-nomic development (Vavrus, 2002c). Seeking greater control over their chil-dren's education, Chagga leaders and parents became more active in schooling during this inter-war period, and they tended to concur with the education-for-development model promoted by the British as World War II approached.

During the 1920s and 1930s, missionaries and government administrators sought to preserve their notion of the African tribe. For example, in his intro-duction to *The Tribal Teachings of the Chagga, Vol. 1*, German missionary Bruno

Gutmann presented his idealized vision of the Chagga tribe: "Once upon a time the tribal teachings really saturated the small Chagga nation like sap of a tree, and created in every individual a more or less evident sense of responsibility toward the greater continuum to which his life was linked" (1932, p. 1). Gutmann and other missionaries of his day were concerned about what they saw as a decline in respect among young Chagga women and men for the authority of traditional leaders. For instance, Gutmann recounted a story about several Chagga chiefs who complained to the colonial authorities regarding obstinate girls in their chiefdoms, girls who were refusing their pre-marital duties and who "also ridiculed the older people and sang songs in which they satirized the connubial woes of the married people" (1926, p. 58). Gutmann argued that this incident was "a sign of decay" due to the influence of foreigners and foreign institutions in Kilimanjaro, and he warned that the "race" would suffer "wherever the old sib discipline disintegrates" (ibid.).

**Figure 1: Students at Mbali Primary School in 2002
Putting on a Chagga *Ngoma*, a Drum and Dance Performance**

In contrast to the German missionaries, who were interned and then expelled by the British in 1916, the American missionaries from the Evangelical Lutheran Augustana Synod of America who came to take their place were inclined to promote adaptation instead of preservation (Vavrus, 2002c). According to Rogers, the American Lutherans had neither the extensive knowledge of Chagga vernacular languages that the Germans had developed nor the "preservation obsession" regarding Chagga culture (1972, p. 436). The American missionaries tended to see the social and economic changes in Chagga communities as a normal part of the development of African societies, so they did not object to Chagga Christians adopting European names and clothing styles and participating actively in schools and churches.

While the colonial government continued to organize schools around tribes, one can discern a shift in educational policy from the late 1920s to the mid-1940s from preserving tribal customs to condemning them. Colwell (2001) aptly describes this dominant binary in colonial education and health policy as "culture-as-cure" and "cultures-as-cause" (p. 14). For instance, the government was quite concerned with low fertility and high infant mortality rates, problems that might lead to an inadequate supply of labor for colonial enterprises. The cultures-as-cause perspective placed the blame for these problems on African women's poor knowledge of hygiene and mothercraft as well as on unhealthy sexual practices among the natives. Foreshadowing—yet also inverting—contemporary population discourses, the solution to the underpopulation problem was to increase schooling for girls at government schools. In a 1927 letter to the Acting Director of Education in Dar es Salaam, Charles Dundas, a colonial administrator in Kilimanjaro and elsewhere in Tanganyika, argued that the low birthrate, one of "our foremost problems" in Tanganyika, could be solved by promoting girls' education:

> In conclusion I would say that by education of the women alone can many of our foremost problems be solved. It is the ignorance of the woman which keeps the African back, it is largely due to their ignorance that hygiene in the African home is so deplorable and it is above all due to their unenlightened ways that the birthrate is greatly below what it could be and that infant mortality deprives the country of a good portion of the population it so sorely needs. Relatively speaking the consequences of ignorance among the men are slight and it is therefore no exaggeration to say that by restricting education to the male sex we are straining at a gnat and swallowing a camel. (1927, pp. 3–4)

By the mid-1930s, colonial reports regularly emphasized the importance of schooling for girls in moving African societies away from cultural practices no longer deemed appropriate and toward European ideas about progress and modernization (Vavrus, 2002c). However, these reports ignored crucial aspects of socioeconomic life in many African communities, such as women's role in agriculture, and did not make them part of the curriculum in colonial schools. Moreover, the increasingly vocal demands of Chagga leaders for more schools for boys and girls were not always heard by colonial officials, who often were attending to other political and financial concerns.

In Old Moshi, Chief Abraham, a descendent of Chief Rindi, actively supported a government proposal to build a prestigious Central School in his chiefdom (Stahl, 1964). The school, which was built on the site of the former German *boma*, was one of only six government central schools for the entire Tanganyika Territory (*Report*, 1926). However, it took much longer to get a response to Chagga demands for a government girls' school, which was finally built after World War II in the Machame chiefdom in western Kilimanjaro (Vavrus, 2002c).

The lack of support from the government for many local development projects motivated Chagga leaders to begin them on their own authority. In addition to building and financing their own schools, these leaders also helped to form a coffee cooperative for Chagga farmers. In 1925, Joseph Merinyo of Old Moshi assembled a group of Chagga coffee growers who had been elected by Chagga farmers throughout Kilimanjaro, and they formed the Kilimanjaro Native Coffee Planters Association (later known as the KNCU). The meeting was significant because it was the first time that Chagga leaders from around the region had come together in such a forum (Rogers, 1972). The union was supported by some British administrators, notably Charles Dundas, and its system of profit distribution—known as "second payment"—helped make the Chagga "the best-off farmers in the country" (Coulson, 1982, p. 65). During good years, the second payment from coffee sales allowed Chagga communities to fund their own Native Authority (NA) education and health projects. However, colonial officials still "held the purse-strings on recurrent and discretionary spending, set the salary rates, and 'advised' the [Chagga] chiefs on the appropriate development projects" (Colwell, 2001, p. 513).

After World War II, Chagga leaders were even more insistent about their dissatisfaction with mission schooling and their desire for more government and NA schools in Kilimanjaro. The call by some Chagga leaders for greater secularization and Africanization of the school system was similar to the sentiments expressed by international organizations, such as UNESCO, and by some officials within the British administration of Tanganyika who saw that independence lay ahead for its African colonies. By the late 1940s, mass schooling was seen as a way to prepare Tanganyikans for citizenship under the system of "responsible self-government" (Buchert, 1994, p. 50).

Despite the growth in government-sponsored secular schooling in Tanganyika during the post-war period, some Chagga parents and leaders were still unhappy. They opposed the government's Ten Year Educational Development Plan of 1948, which sought to promote schooling in underserved parts of the country before allocating more funds for Kilimanjaro. Compared to the rest of Tanganyika, the area was indeed well endowed with educational resources. For instance, the Northern Province, to which Kilimanjaro belonged in 1948, ranked seventh in population but second in the percentage of children enrolled in primary school (Maro, 1974); moreover, there were 72 primary schools in Kilimanjaro at that time, and 57% of Chagga children attended. Still, it angered many Chagga that the government refused to make the Central School in Old Moshi into a senior secondary school by adding Standards 11 and 12 to the existing course of study (Rogers, 1972).

By the end of the colonial era in Tanganyika, schooling for boys and girls had become an integral part of life in Kilimanjaro. Even though Chagga parents seemed to prefer secular schooling for their children at either government or NA schools, mission schooling remained popular for primary education. Moreover, there did not seem to be a conflict for most Chagga in simultaneously supporting secular schooling and either the Lutheran or the Catholic church.

In addition to the spread of Christianity, there was also significant population growth in Tanganyika, and in Kilimanjaro in particular, during the post-World War II period. The 1948 census indicated that the African population of Tanganyika had increased by nearly 50% since the previous census in the early 1930s, and the censuses that followed through the late 1980s continued to show steady growth rates (Colwell, 2001). In the Northern Province, which included Kilimanjaro, the population increased by almost 30% from 1948 to 1957, with the Chagga exhibiting a particularly high rate of growth during this period (Setel, 1995).[2] Increasingly, schooling was seen as the best, or perhaps the only alternative for the middle sons who, because of inheritance customs, were unable to obtain a *kihamba*. For Chagga girls, too, schooling opened up job opportunities, primarily as teachers and nurses who were needed throughout the country, and it may have enhanced their social standing and marriage prospects as well.

The Postcolonial Era

At the time of independence in 1961, there was a serious shortage of Tanganyikans in almost all professional fields because of the small number who had attended post-primary schooling during the colonial period.[3] Those who had had the opportunity for tertiary education were almost exclusively male, primarily the sons of chiefs and of well-educated parents who had studied at Makerere College in Uganda or overseas. Upon independence, the Tanyganikan African National Union (TANU) government, under President Julius Nyerere, developed a Three Year Development Plan for 1961–1964 designed to combat the shortage of Tanzanian professionals. Although Tanzanian in name, the plan was based primarily upon the views of the World Bank and the United States Agency for International Development consultants who worked on it (Coulson, 1982). This plan, focused on manpower development, was followed by a Five Year Plan from 1964–1969 that encouraged the further development of a capitalist economy, with farming and production for the export market remaining in private hands (Samoff, 1990). During this period, the TANU government (later the *Chama cha Mapinduzi*, CCM, the Party of the Revolution) also abolished school segregation on the basis of race or religion (in 1962), eliminated secondary school fees (in 1964), and implemented a regional quota system for entrance into Form I of secondary school (in 1966) in an attempt to equalize the number of students from each region in government secondary schools (Malekela, 1983).

Despite these efforts, however, it was clear by 1967 that the regional and class disparities inherited from the colonial era were still largely intact. In February of 1967, therefore, Nyerere announced a critical shift in the country's development philosophy in a policy statement known as the Arusha Declaration. This "blueprint for socialist development" had four major components: (1) the nationalization of large parts of the industrial sector; (2) the end to private accumulation of wealth by those in the government; (3) priority to the development of rural areas; and (4) the establishment of *ujamaa* ('familyhood' or 'African socialism') by building villages to promote communal agricultural production (Hyden, 1980, p. 96). The Declaration provided for an expanded role of the state in the economic sphere, and by the mid 1970s, almost two-thirds of the wage-earning jobs in Tanzania were controlled by the government (Tripp, 1997).

In March of 1967, Nyerere set forth the educational component of his *ujamaa* program in a policy statement entitled *Education for Self-Reliance* (ESR). The purpose of ESR was to reduce regional, ethnic, and class inequalities in the school system through a revisioning of primary school education. Nyerere argued that primary schooling should become "a complete education in itself," teaching children the practical skills and the appreciation for collective farming that Nyerere believed characterized—or had once characterized—traditional life in rural Tanzania (Nyerere, 1967b, p. 61). Primary schooling was to instill a "former attitude of mind," a precolonial attitude based on unity and community (Nyerere, 1962, p. 6). In particular, schools at the primary and post-primary levels were to become economically self-reliant through farm and workshop projects (Nyerere, 1967b).

Self-reliance (*kujitegemea*) was an important part of Nyerere's vision of socialist development. Self-reliance, he believed, should extend from the level of the self to the level of the Tanzanian state, which would then advocate non-alignment and independence from foreign countries:

> If every individual is self-reliant the ten-house cell will be self-reliant; if all the cells are self-reliant the whole ward will be self-reliant; and if the wards are self-reliant the District will be self-reliant. If the Districts are self-reliant, then the Region is self-reliant, and if the Regions are self-reliant, then the whole nation is self-reliant and this is our aim. (1967a, p. 34)

To promote self-reliance, the government emphasized public schooling. From 1967 to 1979, the number of students enrolled in schools at all levels increased, with a marked rise in primary school enrollments—just as one would expect given the ESR policy of 1967. The government nationalized all schools in 1970, with the exception of a few private secondary schools (Maro, 1974). A program of free universal primary education started in 1974, and in 1978 Nyerere took a further step toward reducing economic inequalities in education by restricting the expansion of private schools in the country. Hoping further to discourage private schooling, he also prohibited students from transferring to a public school after attending a private one (Malekela, 1983). As a result of these efforts to increase primary schooling, enrollments rose from approximately 903,000 children in 1971 to 3,500,000 by 1981 (World Bank, 1999).

Despite the general enthusiasm in the country toward socialist development in the late 1960s and early 1970s, many of the goals of *ujamaa* were unmet because of an array of social and political-economic problems. In the area of education, the goal of becoming self-reliant was never fully realized; for example, even during the height of the *ujamaa* period in the late 1960s and 1970s, foreign financial contributions to the educational development budget were estimated at between 13.9% for 1967/68 and 87.1% for 1976/77. Bilateral funding came largely from Sweden, Denmark, and Norway, and multilateral aid was provided by the World Bank and UNICEF (Samoff, 1990).

Unlike some regions of the country, Kilimanjaro greeted Nyerere's *ujamaa* policies with limited enthusiasm. Because of the high population density on the mountain and the consequent lack of available land there, the government set up *ujamaa* villages on the plains below the mountain and tried to recruit Chagga to move down to populate them. These efforts largely failed, however, because even the poorest households didn't need, or feel that they needed, the services the government was offering. On the mountain they had their families, and this network often provided support during hard times (Howard & Millard, 1997).

Compounding these ill feelings toward *ujamaa* in Kilimanjaro was the economic crisis that hit Tanzania in the 1970s as a result of the high cost of petroleum, a costly war with neighboring Uganda, and a severe drought (Howard & Millard, 1997; Shao, 1992). These problems meant that the cost of petroleum-based fertilizers and pesticides increased while the country's infrastructure worsened, making it more difficult for Chagga farmers to grow and transport their crops (Howard & Millard, 1997). Moreover, because the country needed foreign currency during the *ujamaa* period, the TANU government made it illegal for coffee farmers to uproot their coffee trees even to grow food crops during the drought of the mid-1970s. Thus, wealthier Chagga farmers who could still afford farm supplies to grow both coffee and food crops did not suffer greatly during this period, while malnutrition increased among poorer families on the mountain (ibid.).

In addition, many Chagga resented the government's policies restricting access to schooling in privileged regions such as Kilimanjaro. Once the regional quota system was instituted in 1966, there were fewer spots available in government secondary schools for children from Kilimanjaro. This situation was made worse by the restrictions on private schools, which meant that Chagga communities could not use their own funds, as they had done during the British colonial period, to build their own schools. For decades Chagga parents who could not leave their sons land had offered them schooling instead; for these people, the restrictions and quotas meant that one of the paths to prosperity had been blocked (Moore, 1986). As a result, some Chagga parents looked for ways to circumvent the new system by joining the CCM and using their influence within the party for their children's advancement (Howard & Millard, 1997). Others moved their children to regions where, because of lower average scores on national examinations, their children stood a better chance of being selected to a public secondary school. Still other parents used bribery or other forms of corruption to ensure a spot for their children in public schools

Table 3: Number of Public and Private Secondary Schools in Mainland Tanzania (1994) and Census Population (1988)[4]

Region	Public schools	Private schools	Percentage of total secondary schools	Percentage of mainland population
Arusha	13	23	7.3%	6%
Dar es Salaam	8	15	4.7%	6%
Dodoma	10	7	3.5%	5%
Iringa	13	32	9.1%	5%
Kagera	9	23	6.5%	6%
Kigoma	4	5	1.8%	4%
Kilimanjaro	15	62	15.7%	5%
Lindi	10	2	2.4%	3%
Mara	8	16	4.9%	4%
Mbeya	8	23	6.3%	7%
Morogoro	13	10	4.7%	5%
Mtwara	9	1	2.0%	4%
Mwanza	12	17	5.9%	8%
Pwani (Coast)	9	4	2.6%	3%
Rukwa	7	5	2.4%	3%

Continued on next page

Table 3 (*continued*)

Ruvuma	10	11	4.3%	3%
Shinyanga	9	11	4.1%	8%
Singida	5	5	2.0%	4%
Tabora	10	10	4.1%	5%
Tanga	11	16	5.5%	6%
Total	193	298	99.8%	100%

(Malekela, 1983). Despite government efforts to reduce regional inequalities in secondary schooling, the data in Table 3 show that the Kilimanjaro Region still has far more educational institutions than one would expect given the size of its population relative to the rest of the country.

While the *ujamaa* and ESR policies of the 1960s and 1970s paid a great deal of attention to economic and regional inequities in Tanzania, there was much less emphasis initially on policies that would alter gender relations and promote girls' schooling. The Arusha Declaration, for instance, appeared to be gender blind by using terms such as "citizen" and "individual" in laying out the principles of *ujamaa*. Women appear specifically in the document only in reference to their hard labor in villages and to the "thousands of women in the towns" who waste their energy "in gossip, dancing and drinking" (Nyerere, 1967a, p. 30). Similarly, the ESR document used phrases like "our children," "our pupils," and "our young people" to describe the targets of the program, and it made only a single reference to gender when it stated that both boys and girls should be involved in cleaning their schools (Nyerere, 1967b, p. 71).

By the late 1970s, government policies did reflect a more concerted effort to introduce programs aimed at improving girls' schooling opportunities. The Nyerere administration started several affirmative action programs, such as lowering the scores girls needed on the Standard 7 exam to qualify for public secondary school, and it instituted a different admissions program for women at the national universities (Mbilinyi, 1998). These programs seem to have been successful in equalizing the percentage of girls and boys in primary and secondary schools, but the results for university enrollment have not been as positive because the government stopped affirmative action programs at the tertiary level in the mid-1980s (ibid.). For example, by 1981, girls made up 50% of the students in primary school and 35% of the students in secondary schools (MOEC, 1982). The figures for primary school enrollment have remained equitable and have improved at the secondary level, with girls now constituting 48% of the students who begin Form I (MOEC, 1999). However, gender inequality in enrollment still exists at the upper levels of secondary school and at the tertiary level, with girls making up only 35% of the Form 6 pupils and even fewer of the university students (ibid.). Thus, the *ujamaa* era was a time of rapid increases in primary schooling for boys and girls, and one of its legacies is the relatively equal number of males and females in O-level studies in the country as a whole. These changes have not, up to now, created equitable enrollment at the A-level and beyond, nor have they significantly reduced regional inequalities in education.

Beyond the education sector, other limitations of the self-reliance program were evident by the late 1970s. The government initially blamed external forces for its economic woes, including bad weather, high oil prices, and unfavorable trade relations with other countries (Rugumisa, 1989). While these were certainly important factors leading to severe shortages of basic goods, there were also internal economic and political problems that the government was slowly beginning to admit (van de Walle, 2001). The first economic restructuring program, the National Economic Survival Programme initiated in 1981, set targets for food production and export crops for each region in Tanzania and called on the citizenry to increase their labor output (ibid.). This program had very limited success in curbing inflation and increasing productivity, so in 1986, after the resignation of President Nyerere in 1985, the government adopted an Economic Recovery Programme agreed upon by the government of the new president, Ali Hassan Mwinyi, and the International Monetary Fund (IMF). Subsequent structural adjustment programs (SAPs) continued and expanded these policies of reducing government expenditures, controlling interest rates, allowing for greater private foreign investment, and devaluing the shilling, Tanzania's currency (Shao, 1992).

After nearly two decades of these economic changes, the results suggest that SAPs have improved macroeconomic conditions in the country, as the growth rate now stands at 4–5% per year; inflation has declined considerably to approximately 6%, and irregularities in the foreign exchange market have been eliminated (UNICEF, 2000b; van de Walle, 2001). However, some analysts point out that the devaluation of the shilling has hurt Tanzanian citizens: The value of their currency has declined from 15.3 shillings to $1US in 1984 (TGNP, 1993), to approximately 600 shillings to $1US by the end of 1996, to around 1,000 shillings to the dollar in 2003. Concurrently, the minimum monthly wage (at constant 1970 values) has declined from over 200 shillings in 1972 to below 50 shillings for 1993, while the cost of living index for urban dwellers (at constant 1977 [1977 = 100] values) has increased from 47.9 in 1972 to 3,669.7 in 1993 (Bureau of Statistics, 1995). Moreover, the liberalization of the agricultural sector has led to an increase in prices for farm inputs and the removal of subsidies for fertilizer in Kilimanjaro and elsewhere in the country (Ponte, 1998). These factors, coupled with the precipitous drop in the price farmers receive for a kilogram of coffee—from 1,000 Tanzanian shillings in 1998 to 500 shillings in 2000 (in Kilimanjaro)—are some of the reasons *maisha magumu* has become such a common topic of conversation today (Maarifa ni Ufunguo, 2001).[5]

An additional hardship for many Tanzanians is the closure or sale of parastatal industries to private investors. This privatization effort has obviously saved the government countless shillings and improved efficiency, but it has also left thousands of Tanzanians without a paycheck (Heilman, 1998). According to Jumanne Wagao of the University of Dar es Salaam, the number of public sector jobs plummeted during the second half of the 1980s because SAPs "were biased against employment creation and retention" (1990, p. 27). It was in this context that people in large numbers began to turn to the informal economy for ways to earn a living. The ability of the informal sector to absorb many new traders and service providers may be one of the reasons for the muted public protest to the layoffs, closing of industries, and decline in new jobs during the late 1980s and early 1990s. It is possible that "workers were simply too preoccupied with survival through informal means to protest. They believed the government would have little to offer them in the way of higher wages and saw any move to make such demands as pointless" (Tripp, 1997, p. 101).

In the area of education, SAPs have increased the responsibility of parents and guardians to cover the costs of children's schooling, as privatization and cost sharing programs have expanded in recent years. The government's current education policy, the 1995 *Education and Training Policy*, states: "This [funding] situation calls for a more effective financing plan in which emphasis is redirected more at cost sharing and cost recovery measures with NGOs, private organizations, individuals and communities" (MOEC, 1995a, p. 90).

One strategy the government has implemented to reduce its costs in the education sector is to remove the restrictions on private secondary schooling imposed during the *ujamaa* years. Another is to increase the education-related expenses covered by students at public secondary schools; as early as 1993, public school students were expected to pay for their own uniforms, school supplies, and bedding in addition to modest fees, and more recently, the costs of transportation and some food expenses have also been added to the list of students' contribution (World Bank, 1999). Midway through my fieldwork year in 1996, the government announced that the fees for public secondary school students would rise immediately from 15,000 ($26) to 40,000 ($69) shillings per year for boarding students, and from 8,000 ($14) to 20,000 ($35) shillings for day students (Kitururu, 1996, p. 1).[6] It also announced an increase in the maximum amount that private secondary schools could charge—a fee schedule which is set by the government. Therefore, at the private Njema Secondary School, fees were already 60,000 shillings (approximately $104) for day students and 80,000 (approximately $140) for boarders, and these fees also rose during the middle of the year. Students were then abruptly sent home to collect the additional fees; some never returned to school.

The changes in public and private enrollment patterns from the early 1960s to the mid-1990s can be seen in Table 4. These figures show the steady increase in primary school enrollment after the ESR policy was put into place, and they also illustrate the large increase in private secondary schooling after the mid-1980s.

Although public secondary school students face many challenges, the young women and men at private schools are in an even-greater bind because the fees are far higher and the quality of education is generally considered to be lower (Swainson et al., 1998). The cost and quality problems weigh heavily on the minds of many private secondary school students, who must compete with their public school colleagues on the national exam to obtain a spot at the prestigious national university. The frequent disruption of their studies to collect school fees places students at private schools at an even greater disadvantage, especially the young women and men whose families are barely able to keep up with rising costs. Because most secondary schools in Tanzania are now private institutions, the problems facing these students and their families deserve careful attention. We will consider some of these concerns in the chapters that follow.

Table 4: Student Enrollment in Public and
Private Primary and Secondary Schools, 1961–1994[7]

Students in Primary Schools (in thousands)			Students in Secondary Schools (actual numbers)		
Year	Public	Private	Total	Public	Private	Total
1961	486	39	525	11,832	4,849	16,681
1966	741	48	789	23,836	3,786	27,622
1971	903	19	922	32,603	10,749	43,352
1976	1,874	80	1,954	39,947	17,196	57,143
1981	3,531	8	3,539	38,292	29,310	67,602
1986	3,156	3	3,159	43,363	48,279	91,642
1991	3,507	5	3,512	73,946	92,866	166,812
1994	3,793	3	3,796	83,441	102,805	186,246

Conclusions

Secondary schooling has changed considerably during the decades covered in this chapter. It was once restricted to the sons of chiefs, but it is now available to young men and women who perform well on the national exam and are chosen for a public school. For those who are not selected, the private secondary school system provides an alternative route to a post-primary education. The rapid expansion of private schooling since the mid-1980s increases the size of the educational 'market' where, in theory, all are free to compete. In practice, however, the high cost of private schooling means that it is not and cannot be a choice for the majority of Tanzanian families, whose annual income could not cover the fees and related expenses. If private schooling is too expensive for most Tanzanians and its quality often lower than public schooling, why doesn't the government curtail its expansion and find ways to increase the number of public secondary schools to improve educational equality among wealthy and poor households in the country?

One answer to this question is that policymaking in Tanzania exemplifies the postcolonial condition, whereby 'national' policies in the Third World often reflect the priorities of international financial institutions that issue loans and other forms of development assistance. For example, the 1995 *Education and Training Policy* for Tanzania is based upon neoliberalism and its embrace of the market even though the document contains the occasional reference to the earlier era of education for self-reliance. Samoff argues that this condition reflects the country's shift to greater dependence on NGOs and international organizations like the IMF and the World Bank, thus creating greater reliance on the development models of foreign educational advisors:

> Education policy-making in Tanzania is not a solely Tanzanian activity. Like their colleagues elsewhere in Africa, Tanzanian policy-makers look to the North Atlantic for models, analyses and diagnoses, and approval. Often subtle, this deference to external authority conditions policies—from specifying what is problematic to designing intervention strategies to evaluating outcomes. Even more important, most new projects in education and even a portion of recurrent expenditures rely on externally provided funding. (1994, p. 143)

The vestigial inequality between North Atlantic and African countries is one important part of the postcolonial picture, but so too is the recognition by many Tanzanians that *ujamaa*—socialism in one country—was not the solution to the country's disadvantaged position within the global economy. In Kilimanjaro, for example, Chagga who had benefited from international trade through the sale of their coffee had little interest in collective agricultural endeavors in distant villages. Instead, they appreciated the benefits that global capitalism brought to them even if they rejected some of the cultural changes it ushered in. In the next chapter, we will look at some of these changes in relation to sex education, desires for smaller families, and *maisha magumu*.

NOTES

During most of the period covered in this chapter, the mainland of present-day Tanzania was known as Tanganyika. This name was used by German and British colonial officials to describe the land extending from the border with Kenya in the north to Mozambique in the south and from the Indian Ocean inland to Lake Tanganyika. In 1964, Tanganyika united with the island of Zanzibar to form the United Republic of Tanzania, the country's official name today.

1. See Wright (1968) for a thorough analysis of German colonial education policy, especially with reference to the medium of instruction. She vividly describes the conflict between German administrators, who established an official Swahili curriculum, and missionaries, who opposed this 'Muslim' influence in the schools.

2. Colwell (2001) makes a strong case for interpreting Tanzania's pre-war and post-war census data with caution. She contends that development discourses about the population 'explosion' of the 1950s and 1960s underestimated population growth during the colonial era. Summarizing her well-founded arguments, she states, "When colonial subjects are viewed as wealth producers, I argue, they are too few; when they are viewed as dependents in a future commonwealth, they are too many" (p. 568).

3. For example, there were very few civil engineers (1 Tanganyikan/61 Europeans), physicians (16 Tanganyikans/108 Europeans), and lawyers (2 Tanganyikans/44 Europeans) (Coulson, 1982).

4. The data in this table come from two sources: the *1988 Population Census: Preliminary Report* (Bureau of Statistics, n. date); and the *Basic Education Statistics in Tanzania (BEST): 1994 Regional Data* (Ministry of Education and Culture, 1996).

5. Cooksey (2003) notes even lower prices for coffee than I was quoted in Old Moshi: 200 Tanzanian shillings per kilo or, at the current exchange rate, approximately 20 cents.

6. These dollar amounts are estimates based on the exchange rate at the time of 575 Tanzanian shillings to one dollar.

7. The figures for 1961–1991 come from the Bureau of Statistics (1995), while the figures for 1961–1991 come from the Ministry of Education and Culture (1995a).

Chapter 3

"Condoms Are the Devil" and
the Culture-as-Cure Conundrum

Fieldnotes, August 4, 1996: I had mixed feelings seeing Miss Mlay, my friend and fellow teacher, get married today. We have spent considerable time together at Njema in 1993 and 1996, and I just hope her husband appreciates her good sense of humor and outspoken nature as much as others do....At the wedding the students did a lot of the work to set up the reception hall at Miss Mlay's church in Moshi and to serve the pilau, sodas, and cake to the guests after the ceremony. Some of the female students sang together as a choir, and one Form 4 girl started two songs spontaneously, as other women did at different points while we were waiting for the bride to arrive. However, the lighthearted spirit of the reception was a contrast to the wedding itself and to the minister's sermon on the evils of condoms. The title of a dissertation chapter could be "Condoms ni shetani" [Condoms are the Devil] as he repeated this phrase several times during the service. He kept warning us about the evils of having a girlfriend or boyfriend when one is married, or living together—especially with children—and not married. He seemed to feel that condoms have no place in a marriage because couples will undoubtedly be devoted to each other. Furthermore, condoms should have no other place in society because using them assumes that one is having pre-marital sex. He said in the same breath, however, that AIDS is a big problem and that it is God's punishment for immoral behavior.

The sermon at Miss Mlay's wedding was one of many events during fieldwork in 1996 that clued me in to the complexity of the role of schooling in promoting reproductive health and lower fertility. On the one hand, Miss Mlay fits the profile of the educated woman who is leading the demographic transition in some parts of the Third World: She postponed marriage until her late 20s to complete postsecondary schooling; she was 'empowered' by her education, found a job as a teacher, earned an adequate salary for a single person, and planned to have no more than three children because she wanted to be able to afford schooling for them all. On the other hand, Miss Mlay's marriage to a conservative Christian, whose minister railed against condoms and whose own views on his wife's continued employment were unclear, raised questions for

me about the *women's education* = *empowerment* equation in contemporary population and development policies. Although participant observation at Njema Secondary School helped me see the flaws in this simplistic formula, it has taken
several years of additional research to understand the complex local calculus of
family planning and fertility decline.

This chapter argues that schooling is a less important part of that calculus
than development observers, eager to solve the problem of overpopulation,
often like to believe. To begin with, there is the difficulty of the Tanzanian curriculum, where prescribed biomedical lectures on reproductive health are often
poorly understood because of the educational language policy that requires
English, rather than Swahili, as the medium of instruction in secondary schools
(Vavrus, 2002b). Compounding this point is a second one: Tanzanian schools
are not always very efficient purveyors of information because of the religious
beliefs of teachers (and teacher-ministers) who admonish students not to use
birth control or have abortions. Given these weaknesses, schooling in postcolonial Tanzania, try as it might, cannot be the *primary* reason for the fertility
decline underway in several regions. Although the formal curriculum is no
doubt part of the reason for fertility decline in the Kilimanjaro Region, the final
section of this chapter presents another part, one that is not so easy to cele-
brate: *maisha magumu.*

The Complexity of Culture: Whose Tradition? Whose Past?

The previous chapter examined the writings of missionaries and colonial administrators whose views about Chagga social life shaped education policies and
programs during the first half of the twentieth century. Even though scholars
have raised questions about the accuracy of influential European chroniclers of
Chagga history (Colwell, 2001; Moore, 1996), the names of Charles Dundas and
Bruno Gutmann are still used as reference points when older people discuss the
decline in 'traditional' values and practices. One poignant example comes from
an interview with Mr. Mosha, a Chagga education official in Kilimanjaro. When
I asked his opinion about whether family planning should be taught in secondary schools, he requested that I turn off my tape recorder. He then launched
into an impassioned historical account of the problem of pre-marital sex in
Tanzania today:

Mr. Mosha believes that the problem of girls getting pregnant at school, and of premarital sex more generally, began when "you people"—Americans like myself—arrived in Tanzania in the late 1960s to teach in the Peace Corps program. The Peace Corps volunteers, he tells me, brought books, magazines, and movies that displayed a moral code tolerant of public displays of affection. These Peace Corps volunteers had sex in Tanzania even though they weren't married, and they even had sex with some Tanzanians. Today, Mr. Mosha laments, Tanzanian youth see videos and read books that are quite different from when he was young. Unlike youth today, Mr. Mosha says he never considered pre-marital sex. He believes Tanzanian society has been thrown off its traditional course by the influence of American culture, but now there are efforts being made—through the church and other institutions—to return to the past or to change the path that Tanzanian society is currently on.

As far as family planning is concerned, Mr. Mosha tells me that traditional Chagga culture included a form of family life education as part of the circumcision experience and the preparation for marriage.[1] First, when a girl was circumcised, she and her age cohort were segregated and taught women's roles, including strategies for thwarting men's sexual advances. Second, three months before the consummation of the marriage, a bride was brought to her future husband's home, and female members of his family would teach the woman how to practice birth spacing and other important family life information. Mr. Mosha explains that in the past, it was rare to find a Chagga woman with more than four or five children born closer than 1½ to 2½ years apart. This spacing was achieved through traditional education, he tells me, not through the use of condoms and pills as one finds today.

Mr. Mosha complains about foreigners, with the exception of the culturally sensitive Dr. Bruno Gutmann, because they came and said that female circumcision was heathen and immoral. The foreigners said that other forms of birth control should be used, so today the two traditional periods of family life education have disappeared. Dr. Gutmann, Mr. Mosha argues, appreciated Chagga culture and developed a more appropriate form of Christianity that meshed with Chagga beliefs about one God and about family life in general. Mr. Mosha states that foreigners today tend to have a "corrupted" view of Christianity which permits them to teach family planning before marriage. (interview, May 28, 1996)

Mr. Mosha's views not only express ambivalence about, even an outright resentment of, the postcolonial condition in Tanzania; they contain an explicit challenge to that condition. The ambivalence regarding foreign assistance, particularly volunteer teachers, is easy to see. The Peace Corps, the British VSO, World Vision, and numerous European and American churches provide teachers to fill classrooms that might, for lack of resources, otherwise remain empty. However, as Mr. Mosha pointed out, the morals of foreign teachers may conflict with local ones. The impact of assistance from abroad is apparent not only in the changing attitudes and behavior of youth but also in people's resentment toward dependence on aid.

The implicit challenge in Mr. Mosha's comments is no less pertinent, especially for international population programs seeking to find "culturally acceptable ways of reaching intended audiences" in the Third World (United Nations, 1995, p. 60). Put briefly: Whose definition of Chagga culture will determine what information is acceptable? Younger Tanzanians, who might have sex with foreign teachers? Or Tanzanians who wouldn't do so themselves but wouldn't care if others did? Or Tanzanians like Mr. Mosha, who clearly does care about preserving a 'Chagga' moral code? For international organizations trying to insert family planning curricula into postcolonial countries, this is a crucial question, one almost impossible to answer from the outside. Definitions of culture differ, but I use the term to describe common beliefs and patterns of living that are consistent but mutable from one generation to another. When contestations arise in a community over the teaching of family planning or reproductive health information, whose view of "culturally acceptable" instruction should prevail? The following examples from church and school illustrate the differences in local narratives about Chagga values that would need to be considered in any project designed to promote culturally sensitive family planning instruction in Old Moshi.

On Sundays, I often attended services at the school chapel because they gave me an opportunity to speak with my students and neighbors, improve my Swahili, and learn about important community events. Over the course of the 1996 school year, I heard sermons by visiting ministers, teachers at Njema, and students at the school. The different messages in these sermons and in many conversations with Tanzanian evangelists and American missionaries made it clear to me that there is not 'a' Chagga Christian voice. However, the frequent rhetorical connections between foreign influence and immorality and condoms and HIV/AIDS suggest that these are important, interrelated cultural concerns for many in the community.

The chapel at Njema was built more than 100 years ago, during the German colonial period. Behind this small structure are the tombstones of the German administrators and missionaries who worshipped here and worked a few hundred yards away at the *boma*, which today serves as the main building at Njema. The size of the congregation varied each week, with an average of approximately sixty students, teachers, and neighbors in attendance. Students who did not attend services at the school chapel might go, if they went anywhere, to the nearby Lutheran, Catholic, or Assembly of God churches in Old Moshi or to the mosque in Moshi. However, with 95% of the population in Old Moshi identifying themselves as Lutheran, the school chapel was a popular place of worship, especially on a special day like the one described below:

Today [March 24, 1996] begins the Year of Children and Youth for the ELCT Northern Diocese. To note this event, Reverend Kituo from another Lutheran church has come to present the sermon at the school chapel. Not surprisingly, Reverend Kituo's sermon is about the struggle of youth to overcome a number of social problems. He begins by telling us that he is particularly concerned about five issues: (1) AIDS; (2) the foreign dress that youth are adopting, especially short skirts for women and a type of silky dress pants for men; (3) the use of skin lighteners, hair straighteners, injections, and pills to look like white people; (4) homosexuality; and (5) smoking marijuana as a way of imitating Bob Marley and the Rastafarians. Throughout the sermon, the Reverend uses the phrases "kisasa" (modern), "wazungu" (white people), and "watu wa Ulaya na Merikani" (Europeans and Americans) in reference to these five social problems. At one point, he asks me, the only white person in the congregation, and a very dark-skinned student, the only Masai student present, to stand up at our pews. He then asks this student and the others in the congregation why young Tanzanians want their skin and hair to look like mine. As he probes the students for an answer, it becomes clear that he believes these "genetic" (in English) changes to one's hair and skin color are scornful of God. The Reverend then adds, perhaps in recognition of my obvious embarrassment, that his intention is not to preach conservatism but rather to remind us that the word of God is our guidepost.

The Reverend allows the two of us to sit down, and he moves to his next point about homosexuality. He again calls on me, this time to define homosexuality for the congregation and to confirm his statement that gays and lesbians can marry in churches in the United States. People seem to gasp as I say "Ndiyo, lakini..." (Yes, but...), and the Reverend cuts me off before I can explain the circumstances surrounding the marriage of homosexuals in the USA. The Reverend uses my statement to warn the congregation that "homosexuality is at our door," and then he joins with another pastor seated next to him, Pastor Tembe, in asking all those who disapprove of homosexuality to raise their hands. As hands go up in the air, the Reverend reminds us that "the Bible says one man and one woman" (in Swahili).

After two hours of being called upon as either the symbol of what is wrong with Tanzania or to confer authority on the Reverend's remarks, I slip out of the chapel and head home full of anger at 'the Church.' It feels as though I have been used by the Reverend to make an impression on the students in a way that the other Njema teacher, a Tanzanian seated across the aisle from me, could not. The Reverend's repeated use of the rhetorical question ""Did you hear the white person?" and the phrase "Even our white teacher says this is the case" only added to his misrepresentation of my statements.

By evening my wrath has subsided, and I am able to reflect a bit more on the morning's events. As we sit down for dinner, I hear someone shouting "Hodi, hodi" (a Swahili greeting) from the porch outside. I get up to greet our guests and find that it is Pastor Tembe, his wife, a neighbor, and her daughter, all of whom were at the morning's church service. After they are seated inside and given cups of tea, Pastor Tembe tells us why they have come this evening. He explains that they wanted to express their dismay with the Reverend's use of me as an example during the service today. They were also angry that the Reverend spoke for over three hours on the topic of the sins of youth, which meant that Pastor Tembe had to rush through communion in order to finish the service by one o'clock. Some people, like this neighbor and her daughter, walked out of the sermon and then returned later to take communion. It seems that the daughter felt self-conscious during the sermon because of the rasta braids in her hair and the short skirt she was wearing. Pastor Tembe's wife adds that she wanted to come and see me this evening because she was afraid my early departure from the morning's service indicated that I was upset. We discuss some of the points in the Reverend's sermon that they disagree with, such as the 'problem' of youth dress, and then we say our good-byes as they depart for home.

The difference in the approaches of Reverend Kituo and Pastor Tembe hint at the significance of local struggles over culture, and these struggles suggest that there is no agreed-upon set of beliefs and practices on which policymakers, however well intentioned, can draw in developing culturally sensitive material. For example, one of the most contentious issues during the 1996 school year was the de facto law, applicable in both public and private schools, requiring headmasters and headmistresses to expel pregnant schoolgirls. According to the Ministry of Education and Culture, "Current practices and regulations, not laws, exist whereby girls who become pregnant are expelled from school and are not given another chance to attend school" (1995b, p. 30). This document goes on to state that such practices need to be changed, and this view was shared by almost all of the headmasters and headmistresses I interviewed. Yet those working in church-sponsored private schools—and the majority of secondary schools in Tanzania are now private (and many are sponsored by the Lutheran or Catholic diocese)—faced a dilemma because they believed church officials and parents would not support them if they allowed a pregnant girl to return to school. The interview below (in English) with one private-school headmaster, Mr. Mwendo, illustrates the confusion and consternation of many school leaders regarding the clash between national policy and local school practice.

Fran: We're talking about girls' education, so maybe I'll continue with this. What does happen to a girl if she gets pregnant while she's a student, and what course of action do you think should be taken?

Mwendo: Well, we're very traditional. When a girl gets pregnant at school, she goes away. She's expelled. It's supposed to be like a taboo. "You cannot get pregnant irresponsibly like that and you cannot go to school." If you allow her to stay in school, then you're teaching bad morals to the girls. That's the standard argument. Um, I have a case, last year when I came here, there was one girl who was being talked around as having had [been] pregnant and she aborted it. And then it was very bad on me because I had just arrived, and this girl had already gotten pregnant. It's not proven but that's what people were saying. She had already gotten pregnant and she had aborted. And then people were coming to me: "Why is she at school?" And I say, "What am I supposed to do? This girl was pregnant. She aborted it. What am I supposed to do?" I called one member of the [school] board, two members of the board actually, one of them an ordinary man and another pastor. I brought them here. I told them the problem and then we interviewed the guardian of this girl. He denied it. We interviewed the girl. She denied it. So finally the pastor and the other board member decided that you have no evidence, so let her continue. But then fortunately maybe for me or unfortunately for her, she decided this year to quit school. She was in Form 3 last year. So that's what's supposed to be. If you're pregnant, you go away.

Fran: How does a school know if a girl is pregnant? Is it hearsay or...?

Mwendo: Mostly it's hearsay because it's a day school....

Fran: Are girls ever given pregnancy tests or that kind of thing?

Mwendo: Yes, at this school we're *supposed* to give [a pregnancy test] at least twice a year, every term once. And actually, it is because of this preparation for the examination the next week, the mock and so on, we're supposed to test them this week. Now we're not going to do it. We shall probably have to do this next July. But my own point of view is we're really with these girls for eight hours, no, let's say ten hours every day. The action of getting pregnant happens outside school. It is very tedious for a teacher to monitor the development of a girl when she's still with parents. So really, somebody somewhere should decide that the responsibility for pregnancy is the parents', not the teachers'. If she comes with a pregnancy to school, with current regulations, then the teacher will have to expel her. But to monitor whether she's pregnant or not, to incur these medical checkups, it's an unnecessary expense to the school. We don't stay with them overnight. So that's my personal opinion.

Fran: I see. What's your opinion about teaching family planning to boys and/or to girls in secondary school?

Mwendo: In primary school they're now introducing some sort of family planning to girls, you see. I think the reception would also be good in secondary school *if* the subject were introduced. Right now we don't have a subject dealing with, you know, these issues. Whether or not the boys will receive it as well as the girls I don't know, but I think they should. There's no reason why they shouldn't receive it as well as the girls. At any rate, the cost of living now is very high and everybody is feeling the pinch here. I know. My young son, for example, you wouldn't tell him to get married tomorrow, oh! He would look at you and say "With what? Where's the money coming from?" So boys are slowly running away from marriage. They're delaying it as much as possible to get money. So if this [family planning] were introduced in schools, then there is a very good case to study it. Costs are high; you cannot afford to have so many children. Number one, you cannot afford to marry so young. So I think the reception would be good at this time. (interview, May 16, 1996)

Mr. Mwendo's comments on higher costs and lower fertility desires were similar to those of most parents in Old Moshi with whom I spoke (see below). Moreover, his views on pregnancy and family planning instruction in school mesh with the preferences of national and international population and development planners. However, the opinions of Reverend Kituo and Mr. Mosha are also 'culturally relevant,' considering the enduring role of the Lutheran church in Old Moshi. Whose views should take precedence in a sex education (also called family life education) program? In the next section, I take a closer look at school practices themselves to see how teachers and students draw upon both scientific and moral/religious narratives in articulating their opinions about family planning instruction and reproductive health services.

What Is Learned in School? Language and Pedagogy in the Classroom

It was not until six years after my interview with Mr. Mwendo that I was able to locate a copy of the national family life education (FLE) curriculum. Although the Tanzanian government began receiving support for this project from the United Nations Population Fund (UNFPA) more than a decade ago, I was hard pressed to find any teachers or school officials in 1996 who were aware of the materials that had been produced. The same year, when I spoke with several professors at the University of Dar es Salaam about the FLE program, they, too, were uncertain about its status. In 2002, it was serendipitous that a colleague of mine teaching in the Arusha Region spotted these materials at his school, even though they were not being used there. They were published in 2001 by the Tanzanian Ministry of Education and Culture but under the sponsorship of UNFPA (MOEC, 2001). The FLE lesson plans and teachers' guides clearly reflect the concerns and assumptions, not to mention the optimism, of their sponsor, the UNFPA.[2]

The FLE program offers an innovative approach to incorporating a broad range of population and development themes into the existing national curricula for appropriate secondary school subjects, such as civics, geography, and home economics. The teachers' guide for Form 3 and 4 civics is especially relevant because it includes all of the major issues discussed in this book, i.e., "The Role of Women in the National Economy" (chapter 1); "Gender Equality and Empowerment" (chapter 2); "Health" (chapter 3); "Life Skills Education" (chapter 4); and "Factors Affecting the Environment" (chapter 5). The remaining four chapters in the guide also deal with pertinent topics, such as the relationship between population growth and the environment, customary law and women's rights, sociocultural barriers to women's reproductive health, and international population and development organizations.

The themes of women's rights and empowerment are central to all of the chapters in the curriculum, including the one on health. Although "Health" is the title of the chapter, the units therein focus solely on reproductive health. Similar to the other chapters, this one begins with a justification for the topic, a list of instructional objectives, and detailed lessons for the four class periods to be spent on health issues. The lessons use brainstorming activities, case studies, short lectures by the teacher, and guest speakers to convey the six "core messages":

1. Reproductive health is a human right.
2. Empowered girls delay pregnancy until physical and emotional maturity.
3. Educate men to respect women and share responsibility.
4. Information is protection.
5. Responsible and safe behaviour can be learned.
6. Sexual health education leads to safer sexual behaviour. (MOEC, 2001, p. 20)

If teachers *were* to use these materials, then their secondary school students would be engaged in small group discussions and brainstorming activities about where to get reproductive health information in their community and why young people are not always privy to it. Students would also hear teachers and guest speakers from reproductive health clinics endorsing the view that "RH [reproductive health] information and services [are] universally accepted as a human right; and that this right extends to young people, men, and women" (MOEC, 2001, p. 24). A student-centered, rights-based approach to FLE, such as the one described in this teachers' guide, would certainly have appeal for population and development planners working with the UNFPA and for some Tanzanian teachers and students as well. However, it hardly resembles the pedagogical approach that is actually used in most classrooms in the country.

The classes I observed at Njema and elsewhere demonstrated the "we teach, they listen" pattern of instruction described in Stambach's study of schooling in northern Tanzania (1994, p. 368). Whether or not FLE becomes part of the formal curriculum in most schools, biology classes will continue to be important sites for reproductive health instruction. Biology teachers, such as Miss Swai in the vignette below, draw upon biomedical information in their lectures on reproduction and health. However, like most teachers of other subjects, there is seldom any deviation from the lecture mode of instruction, and this leaves few opportunities for students to discuss the reproductive health dilemmas they may face. Yet there are other reasons, in addition to the sole reliance on a teacher-centered approach to instruction, to question whether students fully comprehend the lessons presented.

One greatly under-acknowledged problem with the *education-as-panacea* concept is that in many former colonies, the language of instruction is not the language of wider communication (Brock-Utne, 2000, 2002; Serpell, 1993). Tanzania is a case in point: The official language policy states that Swahili is the medium of instruction at the primary level (Standards 1–7), with English taught as a subject. It is just the opposite at the secondary level, where English is the medium of instruction for all classes except the Swahili grammar and literature course (MOEC, 1995a). The level of English proficiency among Tanzanian secondary school students is generally low, however, as has been documented in numerous studies (Criper & Dodd, 1984; Mtesigwa, 2001; Rugumisa, 1989). In addition, a recent statistical report from the Tanzanian Ministry of Education and Culture itself shows a continuation of the pattern in which 70–79% of the students taking the national Form 4 examination receive a Division 4 (lowest division) or fail the exam completely (MOEC, 1999). The reasons for these disappointing results are many; a serious one, according to the Executive Secretary of the National Swahili Council in Tanzania, is "students' low level of understanding of the English language resulting from the weak foundations of the subject in primary schools" (Raphael, 2001, p. 1).

A second problem that many students confront in the classroom and beyond is the lack of textbooks. At most secondary schools I visited, it was only in English classes where all the students had books, and these books were usually limited to class readers provided by the British Council's English Language Teaching Support Project. Therefore, students must rely on the notes and diagrams they copy from the blackboard into their notebooks. When classes are very large and blackboards are marred by chipped paint, it is very difficult to read a teacher's notes from the back of the room. If students have the benefit of boarding at school and swapping notebooks in the evenings, as many male students at Njema were able to do, and if these students are careful, then it is possible for them to construct decent textbooks of their own from which to study. However, day students—and girls, in particular—often leave school after they have completed their late afternoon cleanliness assignments because they have chores to do at home before they can resume their studies in the evening (Vavrus, 1998). If they arrive at home with gaps in their notebooks, then they will be studying from a textbook with missing pages—and in a foreign language, too.

The problems described above were clearly evident in Miss Swai's Form I biology class on the day I visited her school. Standing at the front of more than fifty female and male pupils, Miss Swai led a double-period (80 minute) lesson on venereal diseases—in English, as policy dictates—while trying not to be distracted by the loud squeaking door at the back of the classroom or by the researcher videotaping her class.

Swai: Maybe we shall have the topic concerning venereal diseases, in other words, that is sexually transmitted diseases. Are we together?

Students: Yes.

Swai: Now, I'm sure, I'm sure that at the end of this lesson all of you will be able to mention the kinds of sexually transmitted diseases, the causes of transmission, symptoms, and cure for those venereal diseases. Are we together?

Students: Yes.

Swai: OK, now we're going to start with the introduction of our topic. [The teacher turns to the blackboard and writes "Venereal Diseases" at the top. She then turns to face the students again]. OK, by definition, venereal disease or venereal diseases refers to any kind of disease which can be transmitted through sexual intercourse. Are we together?

Students: Yes.

Swai: Now, can you give me examples of those venereal diseases? Any examples?

An older male student raises his hand and says, "Gonorrhea."

Figure 2: Blackboard at a Private
Secondary School After an English lesson

Swai: Good, we have gonorrhea. Any other examples?

The same student stands and says, "Syphilis."

Swai: Any others?

A boy at the back rises slightly and says, "AIDS."

Swai: Good. These are the major kinds of venereal diseases. And these diseases can be transmitted through sexual contact. Are we together?

Students: Yes.

The lesson continues in this manner for more than 30 minutes, with Miss Swai writing key terms on the board and drawing a diagram of the uterus and fallopian tubes to show how the tubes can become blocked in a woman with gonorrhea. She then asks the students questions about the causes of the venereal diseases they have mentioned and the means of preventing them.

Swai: Now, how can you prevent yourself from being infected with this kind of diseases?

A male student who has already answered several questions stands and reads from his notebook: "Avoid sexual contact with infected person."

Swai: So you can simply avoid sexual contact with an infected person. Whenever you hear or you see that an infected person is having gonorrhea, you can simply avoid him or her in...such...things. [Miss Swai hesitated as she finished this sentence.] Are we together?

Students: Yes.

Swai: OK, any others? Hmm [signaling to the same male student with his hand up].
He reads from his notebook, "They must only live with their own husband or wife."
Swai: Good. That is indeed an advice. People are advised to have only one husband or a
single wife. In doing so, they can prevent themselves from gonorrhea. Are we together?
Students: Yes.
Swai: Young girls and boys, you are advised at least to stay with only one partner. Are we
together?
Students: Yes.
Swai: Rather than staying with more than one partner. In so doing, you can prevent your-
self from getting gonorrhea. Are we together?
Students: Yes.
During the latter third of the class period, Miss Swai writes six questions for review on the
blackboard, such as: "What are the major symptoms of gonorrhea?" and "Mention 4 examples of antibiotics which you know." As she writes the questions, the students become
active as they borrow pens from one another and exchange rulers to mark the margins in
their notebooks, a standard practice in the construction of their 'textbooks.' Up to this
point in the class period, only a few students had copied notes from the board. Instead,
most had been sitting quietly as they watched Miss Swai, or they were intermittently whis-
pering to their classmates seated next to them. After completing the questions, Miss Swai
spent the rest of the class walking up and down the two aisles in the classroom and looking over students' shoulders at their notebooks. The class ended when Miss Swai heard
the bell ringing outside the classroom and walked back to the front of the room.
Swai: OK, attention. Now it's the end of our lesson for today, and I would like the monitor to collect all the exercise books. OK?
Students: Yes.
Swai: Thank you. See you. [Miss Swai walks out the door, and the class monitor begins
collecting the students' notebooks to bring to the teacher in the staff room.] (video tran-
script, November 6, 1996).

While advocates of student-centered teaching would probably question the
efficacy of this manner of instruction on pedagogical grounds, a far greater
problem is simply that secondary school students in the lower grades often do
not understand what their teachers are saying when the material is presented
solely in English. For instance, after this particular class, I asked the monitor to
show me some of the students' notebooks before he brought them to Miss
Swai. The incomplete sentences and gross grammatical errors in the notebooks
were similar to the mistakes I had seen in my Form 2 students' work from their
biology, civics, and English classes. When I would ask my students—in Swahili—to explain a concept that I suspected they did not understand, they frequently could not do so in either English or Swahili. Thus, even though I agree
with Stambach that silence in Tanzanian classrooms often "signified and ex-

pressed students' deference to and respect for their teachers" (1994, p. 376), I remain convinced that silence often demonstrates a fundamental incomprehension. The missed information in Miss Swai's biology class highlights one of the reasons why education cannot be a panacea for population problems: In Tanzania, as in other multilingual countries, students do not always understand the language through which biomedical information is presented.

Even if Swahili were the medium of instruction at all grade levels, schools in Tanzania, as elsewhere, would probably still serve as sites where *mis-information* about family planning is sometimes conveyed. In Kilimanjaro, however, this situation is particularly likely because teachers' cultural and religious beliefs may keep them from discussing this topic openly. As Mr. Mosha alluded to above, instruction about sexual matters used to occur during male and female group initiation, not in the home through conversation with one's parents (Setel, 1999; Stambach, 2000; Vavrus, 1998). Therefore, teachers today, especially at boarding schools, relate to students *in loco parentis* and may find it uncomfortable to discuss family planning with them.

My status as a teacher kept Njema students at a respectful distance when it came to discussing their interpersonal relationships, but my identity as a foreign researcher put some students at ease in talking to me off school grounds about their questions and concerns regarding family planning. At first I was puzzled by the number of female students who wanted to know about the safety of abortion services and whether birth control pills had "effects" [side effects; verb form is "ku-affect" in Swahili/English] on a woman's ability to have a child in the future. These young women had clearly heard stories about the dangers of these different methods, and they were usually eager to discuss these stories in my living room. During an interview with two students at Njema, for example, the topic of pregnancy generated a lengthy exchange, part of which is presented below:

Fran: What do girls do to continue with their studies if they get pregnant while still in school?

Juliet: You can't continue in Tanzania. It's really not easy because if you have gotten pregnant, maybe you will be tested—especially at [name of a nearby secondary school]—but they don't test here. Perhaps girls who are pregnant go and have an abortion, and then they continue in school as usual.

Martha: They usually don't return to school. They leave school directly [after getting pregnant].

Fran: Do their parents know if they have had an abortion?

Juliet: They don't know. The abortion is done in secret.

Fran: Who pays the doctor because I would think that it is expensive?

Both: The boy and the girl together.

Juliet: There's an abortion machine at the hospital.

Fran: A machine?

Juliet: It's there. You can have an abortion with this machine, but I have heard that it is very expensive. There is also traditional medicine, different kinds of medicine, that they use.

Martha: Sometimes these traditional medicines kill people. And there are also chloroquine tablets . . . .

Fran: Chloroquine?

Martha: Yes, it's very strong, and you hurt so much you want to die. If you exceed [the right amount], you can die. You will absolutely die. (group interview, March 20, 1996)

The effects of chloroquine and botched abortions were, sadly, topics that many female secondary school students at Njema and elsewhere knew about from second-hand, or perhaps first-hand, experience. Later in the year, the school nurse at Njema did perform external pregnancy exams on the female students. Afterwards, the young women had a meeting with their female teachers about the proper way to wear their school uniforms to avoid advances from male students that might lead to pregnancy and about the importance of preserving one's good moral character while one is in school (Vavrus, 1998). Miss Mwika, one of the teachers who led the session, had shared her views on teaching students about family planning during an interview earlier in the year. In contrast to most teachers at the school, Miss Mwika identified herself as Roman Catholic:

Fran: So since you began teaching here, the boys and girls haven't been taught family planning?

Mwika: Mmm, but we are all taught about it at these Easter conferences. We go to the Easter conference for three days and we're taught by religious people, [who say] "Don't consent to using birth control pills because they *affect* you a lot." We were advised by the priest just to use *natural methods*, those that are safe. And then the woman grows up well and she is healthy every day....The priest said, "Hey, these family planning pills! They have many *effects*." Really, some women come to find that in the end they can't have children at all, and the reason is that these drugs have eroded the uterus. Therefore, when a woman tries to get pregnant, the fetus slips away because the body has become accustomed to it [as a result of the pills]....

Fran: So you would want girls to know that these birth control pills are bad to use?

Mwika: Mmm, maybe they should be used only when she is married with her husband and there is some problem. But even so, I myself, even though there is
a certain [school] committee that is looking into matters of family planning, I
still would not be able to advise girls to involve themselves in these pills because they are girls. They shouldn't *involve* themselves in matters like these.
They only need to deal with studying. Yes, this is what I would advise them.
They shouldn't use these pills at all because they should be studying. [I would
say], "You are a girl, and if you *involve* yourself in these pills, you won't become a parent." These pills, I don't agree with using them because they have
many *effects*. You will find that people who use family planning pills are sick
every day. So what is it for?

Fran: And have you heard of women who have this problem every day?

Mwika: I've heard it. You hear they hurt a lot. I would advise them to just use natural
methods, *natural methods*, just those that use *biology*, just that method of looking at the days [calendar method]. Yea, just this method. And this allows a
woman to live healthfully and not to have any *effects* at all on her body. Because everything she uses in terms of *family planning program* makes her sick. If
she uses it, she gets sick. (interview, April 15, 1996)

The interview with Miss Mwika illustrates one of the ways that schools can be
sites of mis-information about population matters, such as the "effects" of birth
control pills and the reliability of natural family planning methods. In addition
to conversations with their teachers, students hear about these topics from each
other, in casual conversations and in more formal settings, such as the public
debates. At Njema, girls belonged to the debate club, but they rarely spoke. Instead, they listened to what the young men—for some of them, their boyfriends
and future husbands—thought about issues related to land tenure, gender relations, and, in this case, abortion. This particular debate highlights the way young
men use scientific and moral discourses in making arguments about abortion
and abortion in relation to women's rights and difficult living conditions:

Mr. Mabala, a teacher at Njema, welcomed all the students and made general remarks
about the importance of debating and the need for better organization in preparing
such events in the future. Mr. Kibo, another teacher, made a few remarks about how
debating improves students' English skills. The third person to speak was the temporary student chair of the debate club, who explained the two-minute-per-speaker rule
and read the motion: "Abortion should be legalized."

Proposer #1 defined abortion and listed the reasons for making it legal: 1) unwanted
pregnancies due to rape; 2) "health reasons" when giving birth; and 3) the problem that
"village women doesn't have enough income to support his family."[3]

Opposer #1 defined abortion almost exactly as proposer #1 had done except he added that "they kill it (the fetus) before they remove it." "You're committing murder" was his main argument. He discussed the use of "tablets and equipment" and concluded that "there's no need to control population because there's still a lot of land for us to live."

Proposer #2 said abortion should be legal because "we're helping our sisters from death," and he explained how dispensaries and doctors who do it illegally make mistakes, so hospitals would be better. Our "sisters should continue at school...[they] will be chased away" if pregnant, he said. He also noted that "abortion helps for family planning," and that it's "bad luck" sometimes to have more children than planned.

A point of interruption was allowed from another student, who said that abortion "will stimulate prostitution" and the "spread of AIDS."

A second student said this won't happen. Instead, girls are "chased away from society" when they get pregnant, so abortions "help girls to stay in the society." Also, you may "overload your father" by bringing in more people into his household.

Opposer #2 stated that "abortion simply means murder....it is against the law of God." Another point the student made was about prostitution: "Everyone will be free of doing this adultery," and it will "give some freedoms to our sisters here." Another point, in response to the proposers, was that "population can't be controlled by abortion." A further point of interruption was allowed when Proposer #1 said that birth control pills don't always function properly, so it's "not because they're [women] doing as they like."

The audience was then invited to give their views, and a number of boys (mostly A-level students) did so. Someone in the opposition spoke about religion and human rights—"every organism has the right to live." He was then interrupted by Proposer #1, who asked this fellow directly: "Why do you do sexual intercourse which is against the law?" The student didn't answer and went back to his point about the sanctity of life. Proposer #2 asked this same student, "Why do you have sex with girls" given that "the 6th commandment forbids adultery?" The student responded by saying that he was talking about married couples who could be "killing future presidents and ministers."

Proposer #1 took to the floor again and said that "due to scientific reasons" (he has talked to a doctor, he said) women should have the right to have an abortion to save their lives.

One of the opposers then defined abortion as "flushing out" from the womb. This student called himself an opposer but meant proposer, I think, given his arguments: "Students fail to continue with their further studies" because they get pregnant. "This shows us how the underdevelopment was." He also noted that rape happens and "leads to underdevelopment, too."

A Form 1 student who described himself as neutral said, "It will help the family to decrease the family which is not necessary." He also said that some women depend on prostitution for their living and afterwards need to abort.

Finally, the student chairman was told by Mr. Mabala to wrap things up, so the proposers and opposers were given a chance to summarize their arguments. The leading

proposer challenged the opposers' 'no need to reduce the population' argument because "there's nothing to support life in many areas of Tanzania...the society of Tanzania will die." Also, he said he was arguing for legalizing abortion not only for
students but also for a wife and her husband who don't want any more kids—the "income factor...people are not doing abortion because they want to doing it" (i.e., there's
a need for it). He also said the murder argument is for a woman, "not for an offspring." About increasing prostitution, he said people are doing it "very carefully not to
get pregnant." The opposition responded that "it's still making murder." Another proposer jumped in to say that if there's a limited stock of food, having a lot of kids will
constitute murder through starvation. However, Opposer #2 got in the last word by
saying that "God sends man to fill the country." At that point, the chairman of the debate club thanked the two sides and announced that the proposers had received 20
points and the opposers 19. Everyone clapped, and we were dismissed. (fieldnotes, Oc-
tober 3, 1996)

The students' arguments supporting and opposing abortion rights vividly illustrate the interplay of biomedical and moral discourses about population in
this community. The debate shows how young men's views are informed both
by conversations with doctors and by biblical passages. Their understanding of
the dangers of abortion is also quite similar to Miss Mwika's, especially regarding the risk to a woman's health from a poorly performed procedure. Yet what
is also striking about the arguments presented by the proposers is the link between large families and poverty, or "the income factor," as one student put it.
In the final section of the chapter, I want to contrast the optimistic *education-as-
panacea* concept in the population and development literature with the most
common explanations for declining fertility provided by people in Old Moshi:
the conditions associated with *maisha magumu.*

Difficult Life and Fertility Decline

How might the set of difficult life circumstances—captured in the expression
maisha magumu—promote fertility decline and the use of family planning despite
the frequent admonishment against birth control from some church officials,
teachers, and secondary school students themselves? In interview after interview with young people in Kilimanjaro, I heard about not only the desire for
but also the necessity of having no more than four children because of *maisha
magumu*. These low numbers of desired children are identical to those reported
by Richey (2002) in her research on family planning in western Kilimanjaro.

The young, relatively well-educated women in my study were especially adamant that they would work before getting married so that they could save enough to care for themselves and any children should they wind up divorced. Although female students intended to use their education to gain greater control over their productive and reproductive lives—the very definition of the empowered Third World female—they displayed little of the optimism that characterizes the more theoretical discussions of empowerment found in international development discourses. Instead, they frequently talked about domestic violence and men's abuse of alcohol as reasons why women often have more children than they desire; schooling, they hoped, would keep them from this plight by enabling them to get jobs and raise their few children without a husband in the household should this become necessary.

The consistency in young women's pessimistic interpretation of *education as panacea*, i.e., education as a way to cope with domestic crises, made me curious to see whether their parents shared these views. I wondered if adults in Old Moshi saw a connection between schooling for girls and empowerment and whether they understood empowerment as the ability to cope with negative circumstances, as their daughters did. Or would they define empowerment in the more positive terms of policymakers, whose educated women gain "full participation at all levels in the social, economic and political lives of their communities" (United Nations, 1995, p. 6). In addition, I wanted to know whether young women's lower fertility desires signaled for their parents a cultural crisis and a loss of Chagga identity.

To learn about parents' perspectives, I spent considerable time talking to adults who lived in the villages near the Njema campus. This was done informally during community functions, such as church services and weddings, and in casual conversations while walking along the paths leading from school to market to home. Mr. Moshi and I also conducted formal interviews with adults living in the area to find out what parents thought about the major themes emerging from my school observations and interviews with teachers and students.

The reproductive histories of these adults stand in stark contrast to the fertility desires of their daughters and their own desires *for* their daughters. For instance, it was striking that the adults averaged over eight children themselves but wanted only three or four children for their female and male offspring. This pattern of high actual fertility but lower desired fertility is similar to the findings from Hollos and Larsen's study of Pare adults in eastern Kilimanjaro (1997).

The women they interviewed had had six children of their own but now felt that four children were the ideal, largely because of the costs associated with schooling.

Most of the adults in my study were over 40 years old, but they were not wedded to the idea that large families were central to Chagga identity (Vavrus, 1998). When land was more fertile and abundant, they contended, having many sons and daughters made sense, and sending them to school was not as critical. As one mother explained:

> At that time [1940s and 1950s], the problem was that parents were ignorant of the value of education and, therefore, did not care much about educating their children. Parents were satisfied if their children completed Standard 2 or 3....Parents wanted their children to farm and look after their cattle. (interview, June 24, 1996)

Similar to their Pare neighbors, the Chagga adults in this study reported that the high cost of schooling makes it difficult for them to be 'good' parents unless they have fewer children than in the past. A good parent, they believed, is one who understands the value of formal education and sees to it that his or her children complete, at a bare minimum, primary school. The importance of primary schooling for Chagga parents is borne out in the fact that the Kilimanjaro Region has the highest net enrollment ratio for primary school of any region in the country (81), including the commercial capital, Dar es Salaam, whose ratio is 71 (National Bureau of Statistics, 2002).[4] Providing one's children with a post-primary education is especially valued, but it remains an elusive goal for many parents because of the problems of land shortages and the environmental degradation that have intensified on the mountain during their lifetimes. The comments of two fathers illustrate these widely held views about education and the environment:

> For example, we Chagga right now, as we see, [it's not like] in the past when children were given fields, farms, and whatever. The farms, the fields, we think they have been exhausted. What we now give [a child] is education so that she can further herself. If she has gotten this education, I think this is the inheritance she has gotten from us. (interview, June 11, 1996)[5]

> Actually, today life has become more difficult....First, in some parts of the country, like here on the slopes of Mount Kilimanjaro, many farms are now occupied and worn out. You find an old man like me always working on my farm, but what I reap from this

farm is very little. Furthermore, people have engaged in deforestation for individual economic gains, thus causing the streams to dry up. (interview, June 4, 1996)[6]

The changing physical landscape on the mountain described by these two men is an inextricable part of the materiality of *maisha magumu*. As we will see in Chapter 5, these changes also reflect the postcolonial condition in which development programs for the agriculture and water sectors—promoted both by the national government and international financial institutions—sometimes make it harder for Chagga farmers to earn their livelihood from the land. Yet there is also an ideological dimension to *maisha magumu* that helps explain the connection between girls' schooling and fertility decline in Kilimanjaro. Using positive terms such as "self-reliance" (*kujitegemea*), parents in Old Moshi reveal how the imagination helps to turn collective beliefs about the future into action (Appadurai, 1996): In this community, educating one's daughters is a key marker of cultural identity as a Chagga and as an 'educated person' (Levinson & Holland, 1996). Despite the economic hardships for many Chagga families, their support of girls' schooling is part of the collective imagination that distinguishes Chagga from "those Masai in Arusha" and people in "those regions in the southern part of the country," as several people remarked during interviews. These adults' views suggest that 'good' Chagga parents recognize that schooling is the best way to help one's children cope with *maisha magumu*.

In addition to specific national references about identity and development, some people in Kilimanjaro also drew upon international development discourses in discussing their support of girls' schooling and FLE. For instance, the parents in this study often explained their views by making reference to "the gender issue," "the democratization of family life," and the importance of girls being "independent." In conversations with parents who work with international NGOs, the English term "empowerment" was often used in our Swahili conversations. The sentiments conveyed by these phrases would likely be supported both by the parents' female offspring and by international population and development planners who tend to see women's empowerment as the core of policy reform. However, the concept of empowerment as it appears at the level of 'the global' frequently does not acknowledge the profound strain on local resources that parents feel when their daughters—and sons—are not empowered.

The term *mzigo*—a burden—that parents in Old Moshi often used to explain their reasons for supporting girls' schooling is a case in point. Although parents have different rationales for sending their daughters to school, the frequent use of *mzigo* to describe their decisions about secondary schooling helped me to appreciate the dilemma many of them confront: The current conditions of difficult life place parents in a double bind because to avoid the extremes of *maisha magumu*, one needs to educate one's children—girls and boys—so that they can care for themselves. The high cost of schooling, however, and the toilsome task of farming make it impossible for most parents to provide their children with more than a primary education. Without an education, parents fear that their children will be a burden to them in the future, yet educating them is an onus in the present.

Given the uncertainties of postsecondary school employment today, one might think that this burden on Chagga households—large investment, scant return—would make parents reluctant to keep sending, or trying to send, their children to school. However, rather than losing faith in education for its frequent failure to empower or to employ, parents described a strategy that may be contributing to lower fertility in many parts of the world, namely, to have fewer children but to invest more in each one. The words of one elderly widow and mother of eight shed light on this recent change in parenting practice:

> My husband and I used to share the burden [of raising children], but now I am alone. How I wish God could have spared him a little longer! We could have educated two or three children perhaps....Today if a child is not educated at least to Standard 7, I don't know which prison he will end up in....I feel bitter when I look at this house. Looking around, pity grips you and you say to yourself, "God, why have you brought these children into the world? Will they survive or not?"....This country is full of people who are not getting care at all, who are homeless with virtually no job and no sign of development whatsoever. These are the serious issues that lead people to say, "Life is difficult." (interview, June 5, 1996)

Conclusions

Real problems—both financial and interpersonal—seem to underlie the desire for smaller families among young women and their parents. The imagination, too, is a factor in the incipient fertility decline because the collective, future-oriented vision of many people in the region creates specific ideas of the 'good' parent, i.e., the parent whose children *all* go to school. For most Chagga parents, the only way to live up to this ideal today is by having fewer children than people on the mountain had in the past. Thus, in less than a generation, the interplay of *maisha magumu* and of desires for post-primary schooling has produced the widespread view that smaller families are better than large ones.

To what extent has formal education in schools contributed to this transformation? The examples in this chapter, from the conservative views of school officials to the limited comprehension of students in English-medium biology classes, show that schooling may not provide a young woman with much accurate or accessible information about family planning. Moreover, a secondary school diploma provides no guarantee of a job upon graduation and the empowerment associated with employment. Undoubtedly, women with more education are more likely to understand health-related information about family planning and childhood illnesses and to successfully engage in the verbal interactions demanded of them by the formal health care system (Dexter et al., 1998; LeVine, 1999; LeVine et al., 1991). Yet, as the interview with Miss Mwika illustrated, a secondary school education does not ensure that one grasps the process of contraception or wants to teach about it even if she does.

Secondary schooling is supposed to help combat economic problems, and in the best-case scenarios of international policy documents, it does. But on Kilimanjaro, *education as panacea* does not take account of the lived experience of schooling and the specific limitations on teaching and learning that arise in different cultural contexts. This optimistic concept also fails to recognize the difficult material conditions, intensified by schooling itself, for people who have neither adequate farmland nor adequate income. We look more closely at *maisha magumu* in relation to women's employment and reproductive health in the next chapter as we learn about the events that have transpired in the lives of these Njema students four years later.

NOTES

1. Female circumcision in Africa is a hotly debated topic, but I will not go into detail about it in this book because it was seldom a topic of conversation in Old Moshi. For a discussion of this practice in Kilimanjaro today, see Stambach (2000).

2. For an insightful analysis of the relationship between Tanzania's National Population Policy and international development institutions, such as the UNFPA and the World Bank, see the studies published by Richey (1999, 2001).

3. I have included phrases uttered by the students to indicate their level of proficiency in English. The majority of the students who spoke were in the final two years of O-level studies or in the A-level program.

4. The net primary school enrollment ratio is calculated by dividing the number of children enrolled in primary school who are in the official age group for those grades by the total number of children in the same age group (UNICEF, 1999). The ratio for mainland Tanzania is 59 (National Bureau of Statistics, 2002); the United States, in contrast, is approximately 96 (UNICEF, 1999).

5. The third-person singular pronoun in Swahili (*yeye*) does not distinguish between male and female referents. Therefore, in some cases, it is difficult to determine whether a person is speaking of a boy or a girl when *yeye* refers to the word "child" (*mtoto*), as in this excerpt. Throughout the book, I have alternated "he" and "she" as the translation for *yeye,* but it should be borne in mind that the gender was not specified in the interview.

6. The sentiments of these two men regarding education as inheritance are much like those of Chagga living in western Kilimanjaro, where Stambach (2000) conducted research about schooling, gender, and generational change. She begins a chapter on this topic with an epigraph taken from a graduation speech at a secondary school: "There is no inheritance, we do not have any valuable inheritance that we can give our children that is more valuable than education" (p. 30). The same words could easily have been uttered at a commencement address at Njema Secondary School.

Chapter 4

AIDS and Education in
an Era of Economic Decline

One of the most critical problems facing international development agencies and government officials in the Third World is the HIV/AIDS epidemic. Speaking at the World Education Forum held in 2000 in Dakar, the Executive Director of UNAIDS argued that AIDS "constitutes one of the biggest crises and the biggest threats to the global education agenda that we have known. There is no other single factor in the world today that so systematically undermines the gains of decades of investment in human resources, education, health and the well-being of nations" (Onishi, 2000, p. A1). The epidemic has had especially devastating consequences for school-age children and adolescents in Sub-Saharan Africa, the region where over 70% of the people living with HIV/AIDS worldwide reside. In 1999, for example, 860,000 primary school students in Sub-Saharan Africa lost a teacher to AIDS, and many more children can no longer attend school because they are needed at home to care for ailing relatives or for the children of deceased family members (UNICEF, 2000a).

The empty classrooms and ailing teachers in many African schools make it relatively easy to track the effects of AIDS on children's education, but it is far more difficult to study the opposite: the impact of education on curbing the AIDS epidemic. The studies reviewed by Vandemoortele (2000) from Zambia and Uganda suggest that the more years a woman spends in school, the lower her likelihood of HIV infection. According to the author, the "education vaccine" works through the mechanism of empowerment: Women with more years of schooling have more equitable sexual relations, which allow them to put their knowledge of AIDS prevention into practice (p. 17). The empowerment argument certainly has great appeal in a country like Tanzania, where girls between 15 and 19 years of age are six times as likely to be infected with HIV as their male counterparts (UNICEF, 2000b). Their age and limited education may make it difficult for them to comprehend the implications of the AIDS epidemic for their lives and to act assertively with sexual partners who are reluctant to use condoms. However, the lives of the slightly older female secondary school graduates described below suggest that the education vaccine is not 100% effective.

The previous chapter depicted some of the contradictory messages about condoms encountered by Tanzanian youth in schools and churches as well as the role of *maisha magumu* in reducing one's desired number of children. This chapter takes the analysis one step further by examining the views of secondary school graduates on condom use and sexual risk in an era of AIDS. The young women and men who studied at Njema in 1996 are well educated by national standards in a country of nearly 35 million people where only 21,000 youth make it to Form 4—the final year of secondary school—each year (MOEC, 1999). However, these graduates, especially the young women, seldom use condoms with their partners even though they are familiar with the safe-sex messages on billboards, television, and radio. Although public health education is obviously a crucial first step in reducing HIV transmission, it is not a panacea for slowing the spread of AIDS when economic decline is coupled with a strong desire for further schooling. Farmer, in his research on HIV/AIDS in Haiti, makes a similar argument:

> Educating everyone, and especially the young, is our civic duty, part of being human. But show us the data to suggest that, in settings where social conditions determine risk for HIV infection, cognitive exercises can fundamentally alter risk....We can already show that many who acquire HIV infection do so *in spite of* knowing enough information to protect themselves, if indeed cognitive concerns were ever central to preventing HIV among the poor. (1999, p. xxv; emphasis in original).

Although this chapter does not look at the poorest residents of Old Moshi, it nevertheless reveals how social conditions influence sexual risk. In this case, the conditions include severe limits, even in one of the most prosperous regions of the country, on opportunities both for postsecondary education and for formal employment.

"Talking to the Deaf": AIDS Education among Tanzanian Youth

The limitations of AIDS education programs were made clear to me during focus group discussions in 2001 with Njema graduates who had been my students in 1996. James was one of these students, and he now works for a Christian NGO involved with AIDS education in East Africa. He has traveled widely in Tanzania, Kenya, and Uganda as a youth educator and has grown dismayed by the poor response to the NGO's safe sex message even though it echoes the government's own AIDS education campaign. "When they hear on the radio or see in a magazine that AIDS kills so use family planning to protect yourself, it's like talking to people who are deaf," James told the five of us gathered around a dining room table. He became more animated as he described the meetings he had had recently with students at schools in Kilimanjaro: "At one of these schools, a girl told me that she was more afraid of getting pregnant than getting AIDS. 'If I get pregnant, I will have a problem because I will have a child who has no father,' she said. Or the boys are worried about getting a girl pregnant while they are still dependent on their parents. So I asked them about AIDS, and they said, 'Oh, it's like an accident at work.'"[1] Another Njema graduate, Mary, jumped in: "Yes, they say they will die later." A few minutes later, Mary added her views on the reasons why some girls are especially vulnerable to AIDS: "A big thing that causes people to get AIDS in Tanzania is prostitution. If you ask them why, they will say that they don't like it but they do this to get money. So this decision isn't bad," she said with sympathy, "because they do it to get out of poverty" (focus group, June 10, 2001).

One of the best ways to illustrate the complex interplay of poverty, schooling, gender relations, and AIDS is to trace the trajectories of young people like James and Mary during the first few years after completing secondary school. Their lives have been affected in multiple ways by the political economy of the country and the SAPs the government has pursued since the mid-1980s, especially the policies that have led to increases in the cost of schooling and declines in civil service jobs for secondary school graduates. The complexity of these young people's lives is also revealed in their views on sexual risk that *cannot* be explained solely by a materialist interpretation of their circumstances: Even if Tanzania were a very wealthy country, some individuals would not take precautions to prevent pregnancy and HIV transmission because risk-taking "can have its own unrelenting logic" (Whyte, 1997, p. 22). However, this chapter focuses on the economic hardships that help explain why some young women and men in Kilimanjaro are often more worried about immediate concerns, such as avoiding pregnancy, than they are about the more distant problem of AIDS. Their actions cannot always be reduced to problems of inadequate resources or to insufficient health knowledge as the *education-as-panacea* perspective suggests; instead, they reflect both material and ideological dimensions of the postcolonial condition, which, on the one hand, create a hunger for schooling and, on the other, make it difficult, almost impossible, to satisfy that hunger.

Background to the Epidemic

The AIDS epidemic in Tanzania highlights the role of macroeconomic policies in the construction of sexual risk for young women and men. Just as the era of structural adjustment was beginning, the disease spread rapidly across Sub-Saharan Africa.[2] When the first cases were reported in the region in the early 1980s, it was heterosexual adults with higher socioeconomic status and higher levels of education who were most likely to be infected because they had the greatest opportunities for travel and the financial means to establish relationships with multiple sex partners. Educational campaigns were effective in curtailing, though not eliminating, the spread of HIV infection among adults in this segment of the population (Basu, 1999; Vandemoortele, 2000). Today, HIV infection is increasing most dramatically among young people of secondary and tertiary school age. In Tanzania, for example, 60% of new HIV infections occur among young women and men between the ages of 15 and 24 (UNICEF, 2000b). The demographic shift in infection rates from older to younger persons is also a gendered phenomenon in Tanzania and in other parts of the world; young women are far more likely to be infected than are young men (Simmons et al., 1996; UNICEF, 2000b).

To determine the reasons for the high rates of HIV infection among 15 to 24-year-olds, there have been several studies conducted in Tanzania to assess the level of reproductive health knowledge of secondary school students (Kapiga et al., 1992; Matasha et al., 1998; Mnyika, et al., 1995a). These studies, based on research conducted along the Tanzanian coast, in the northwest near Lake Victoria, and in the Kilimanjaro and Arusha Regions in the north, all demonstrate that knowledge about sexually transmitted diseases does not necessarily translate into the use of condoms. A study by Mnyika et al. (1995b) in the Kilimanjaro Region is particularly important because it shows that condom awareness among 15-19-year-olds was relatively high (51.5%), but regular condom use was only 10%. Most relevant is the finding that the 20-24-year-olds in the study reported even greater knowledge of condoms (72.8%) but also a low percentage of condom use (23.3%). The authors conclude that the two major barriers to teenagers' use of condoms in the region are their misperceptions about their level of sexual risk and the problems they face in obtaining contraceptives at health facilities.

In addition to this study, the 1996 Demographic and Health Survey for Tanzania shows that women who have completed secondary or postsecondary schooling have the greatest knowledge of HIV/AIDS of any group of women in the country, but they are also the ones who are most likely to report that they are at "no risk at all" of contracting the disease. Although they report a slightly increased use of condoms compared to women with less schooling, women who have completed some secondary or tertiary schooling are no more likely to have reduced their number of sex partners or to have restricted their partners to only one in light of the AIDS epidemic (Bureau of Statistics Tanzania and Macro International Inc., 1997).

These studies in Tanzania suggest that knowledge about HIV/AIDS does not necessarily lead to actions that would curb the spread of the disease. Risk-taking among secondary and postsecondary graduates is part of the mystery, or "unrelenting logic" (Whyte, 1997, p. 22), of sexual behavior for which *education as panacea* cannot account. Some anthropological research on AIDS conducted elsewhere in Africa has demonstrated the necessity of considering a range of factors that contribute to conditions of sexual risk, including gender relations, land tenure, poverty, and the global economy (Bond et al., 1997; Farmer, 1996; Schoepf, 1998). In Tanzania, however, there has been little research on AIDS, schooling, and the political economy to see how they interact and affect young people in different regions of the country.

The insightful study by Setel on AIDS and youth culture in the Kilimanjaro Region, however, is an exception to this general trend. As Setel notes, the increased movement of young people from rural communities on Mount Kilimanjaro to urban areas around the town of Moshi is the result of the economic decline that began in the 1980s and spawned the rapid growth of the informal sector as civil service jobs diminished and wages from formal employment eroded. The rise of the informal economy corresponds with the emergence of the AIDS epidemic in Tanzania, but Setel is careful to point out that we cannot necessarily conclude that one of these forces caused the other. Nevertheless, their co-occurrence highlights the interrelationship between macroeconomic conditions and sexual risk: "For young people, this alignment of structural forces proved to be a fatal and paradoxical bit of serendipity. At the moment environmental conditions for youth had reached their worst and many became involved in the black market (*magendo*) and informal sector activities, HIV arrived" (Setel, 1999, p. 147).

The arrival of HIV/AIDS in Kilimanjaro occurred within a specific regional context in which an important urban center—the town of Moshi—has for decades attracted young men and women from nearby rural communities on the mountain, such as Old Moshi. Two historical factors are particularly important in understanding how current conditions of *maisha magumu* and desires for schooling reflect longer-term migration processes in the region. As described in Chapter 2, the relations of production and the rapid growth of formal education at mission and colonial schools profoundly influenced the social and political-economic environment on Mount Kilimanjaro. The British administration encouraged Chagga farmers to grow coffee as a cash crop along with or instead of subsistence crops, a practice that exacerbated land pressure in the fertile middle-altitude belt as the growing of coffee became a desirable occupation (Moore, 1986; Rogers, 1972). In addition, missionaries and colonial administrators acquired many of the remaining unclaimed plots on the mountain for churches, schools, and government offices, thereby reducing even further the land available for subsequent generations of Chagga families (Howard & Millard, 1997; Maro, 1974; Moore, 1986). As land scarcity became a larger problem, men—especially middle sons, who rarely inherit their father's land—began to move down off the mountain and take up residence in Moshi and other cities in Tanzania.

A second historical factor related to current migration patterns is the rapid growth of schooling in Kilimanjaro since the 1920s and the changes in cultural and economic conditions this engendered. The long and sustained history of support for formal education that began with the building of schools by German and British missionaries in the late 19th century continues to the present with the growth of private secondary schools over the past two decades (Stambach, 2000; Vavrus, 1998). Data from the early 1980s show that students from Kilimanjaro were still overrepresented at the A-level of secondary school; for instance, Chagga constitute less than 5% of the national population but 16.5% of the Form 5 students, with Chagga girls making up almost one-third of the total female Form 5 population in the country (TADREG, 1990). Young women and men from rural areas who achieve these levels of education often seek employment in urban areas that they believe is commensurate with their status as educated persons. The alternative, they believe, is to stay in their parents' homes, where, as we saw in the previous chapter, they may feel like a burden (*mzigo*), and like a failure (Serpell, 1993).

In sum, school enrollment rates in Kilimanjaro remain among the highest in the country; opportunities for private secondary schooling are certainly growing, and observers note a "mood of enthusiasm" for educational and economic advancement among some young Chagga today (Stambach, 2000, p. 162). Nevertheless, there are many others who are dismayed by their family's inability to cover the cost of schooling and pessimistic about a future where their educational goals are likely to go unmet.

**Figure 3: Secondary School Girls
Preparing for an Examination**

Life After Secondary School

In 2000, I mailed a questionnaire and essay question to 225 of the women and men who had completed a similar questionnaire four years earlier when they were students at Njema or at another secondary school in Kilimanjaro (see Introduction). For the sake of clarity, I have organized the themes into three categories, but this should not imply that these are discrete topics. Rather, *sponsorship for schooling, employment and idleness,* and *sexual risk* are inextricably interconnected experiences for the young people in this study.

Sponsorship for Schooling

School sponsorship has been examined by a number of researchers interested in girls' education in Africa (Bledsoe, 1990; Bledsoe & Cohen, 1993; Gage & Bledsoe, 1994; Komba-Malekela & Liljestrom, 1994). Bledsoe's research in Sierra Leone suggests that the payment of a girl's school fees by a man other than her father "can signal marital or sexual interest" (1990, p. 286). When boys seek assistance with school fees from someone outside the nuclear family, which is a common practice in both Sierra Leone and Tanzania, there is seldom any expectation of sexual favors implied in the transaction. Furthermore, Gage and Bledsoe note that the economic decline in Sierra Leone has created a context in which parents tacitly acknowledge that their daughters receive school fees from men of wealth or influence in exchange for sex or promises of marriage (1994).

The issue of sponsorship has become a more salient feature in discourses about schooling in Tanzania since the Tanzanian government introduced school fees at public secondary schools and began promoting the expansion of private ones (Samoff, 1987). According to the World Bank, expenses at a private secondary school are 63% higher than they are at a public one, and the relative financial burden is heaviest for the poorest households in the country (1999). Nevertheless, 55% of secondary students today are enrolled in private schools because there are far more of these institutions, and their number continues to grow more rapidly than does the number of public schools (MOEC, 1996). Although private secondary schools may be desirable for youths who do not qualify for the less-expensive public school system, it comes at a high price for students and their families.

The growth of private secondary schooling and the introduction of cost-sharing measures at public schools—both at the primary and secondary levels—highlight the contradictory effects of SAPs at the local level. Although many people welcome the expansion of private schooling in the post-*ujamaa* era, they lament the increase in the cost of living and the reduction in real wages that keep most poor families from taking advantage of schools supported by churches and NGOs. Recent educational statistics are revealing: The proportion of secondary school students whose parents are peasant farmers has declined since the private education sector began to expand in the mid-1980s (Lassibille et al., 2000). Moreover, there is a striking difference between the secondary school enrollment rates for students—male and female—whose families are in the lowest quintile for household expenditures (2%) and for those whose families are in the highest quintile (14–15%) (World Bank, 1999). Although children from poor families still attend secondary school, the rising fees at both public and private schools make it more difficult for them to do so.

The effects of SAPs on the lives of the young people in this study show mixed results. Some of them have found good jobs in the private sector or are now studying at private schools that have far more resources than they could have managed during the *ujamaa* years, when currency exchanges and imports were tightly restricted. However, many others, especially the young women, remain "idle" at home with no regular employment or immediate educational prospects. Only 20% of these former female and male students report that the economy has improved since 1996, and only 13% say they are more satisfied with their lives now than they were four years ago. This sense of dissatisfaction is not as strong as the "overwhelming sense of decline and despair" that Ferguson describes in his "ethnography of decline" in Zambia (1999, p. 12, 20). Rather, the sentiments expressed are similar to those of the students described by Stambach, whose research in western Kilimanjaro revealed "a tenor of disappointment" among many secondary school graduates even though others felt enthusiastic about the future (2000, p. 163).

The sense of dissatisfaction with the current state of affairs compared to 1996 is due, in part, to the respondents' difficulties in finding a sponsor to cover the costs of education beyond Form 4. Data from the 1996 questionnaire revealed two important aspects of the school sponsorship issue that help explain why some former students, especially young women and youths from poor households, feel a sense of despair today that was not evident four years ago. First, in 1996, there were no significant differences between male and female students in the difficulties they faced paying school fees. In fact, the majority of males (62%) and females (66%) reported that they did not have any problems covering the costs of schooling at that time. However, since the middle of 1996, fees at private secondary schools and school-related expenses have risen dramatically. As noted in the Chapter 2, school fees at Njema were 60,000 Tanzanian shillings at the beginning of the 1996 school year (approximately $104); by 2000, they cost an astonishing 175,000 shillings (approximately $220).

And it should be remembered that these increases are taking place in a country with a yearly per-capita gross national product of around $110 and incomes ranging from $538 in Dar es Salaam to $180 in rural areas (World Bank, 1999).

The majority of Njema students were able to pay their school expenses in 1996 because most of them come from relatively prosperous households. Table 5 illustrates some of the differences in household wealth by comparing possessions in the students' households with those in the Kilimanjaro Region and in mainland Tanzania. These indicators of household wealth were compared for the male and female students in the study to determine whether there were differences between them that might affect their enrollment and educational attainment. There were significant differences ($p < .05$) between the number of boys and girls who live in households with electricity and a television, with male students more likely to live in homes with these amenities, but no differences were found between them in terms of piped water in the home or ownership of a car by a family member. The greatest differences, however, are between these secondary school students' families and the majority of households in Tanzania.

Table 5: Household Resources in Mainland Tanzania, the Kilimanjaro Region, and Among Secondary School Students in the Study, 1996 Questionnaire[3]

Resource	Mainland Tanzania	Kilimanjaro Region	1996 Students
Indoor water	12%	13%	72%
Electricity	12%	21%	54%
Television	3%	3%	25%
Motorbike	1%	2%	15%

The second significant set of findings from the 1996 questionnaire concerns the person who paid the students' school fees and how many years of formal education the students' parents had completed. In the study, fathers, or fathers and mothers together, paid school fees for 60% of the boys compared to 40% of the girls. The female students whose fathers did not pay their fees relied on their mothers alone, uncles, or other relatives and friends for these expenses. Although there were no differences in the percentage of male and female students who lived with their father and mother, there were significant differences in the level of education for the boys' and girls' parents. The parents of the male students were significantly more likely to have completed some secondary or tertiary schooling than were the parents of the female students. For instance, 65% of the male students but only 47% of the female students had fathers with some postprimary education. Moreover, 52% of the male students compared to 31% of the female students had mothers who had continued in school beyond the primary level. The data show that the girls were significantly more likely than the boys to have fathers and mothers who had not completed primary school or had never been to school at all.

The quantitative data from the 1996 and the 2000 questionnaires do not permit an analysis of how the differences in household wealth, sponsorship for schooling, and parents' level of education might affect postsecondary school opportunities in Tanzania. However, the essays written in 2000 by these secondary school graduates suggest that SAPs have influenced their lives in a variety of direct and indirect ways. Both men and women wrote extensively about the difficulties they have faced over the past four years in trying to find sponsors to pay their school-related expenses or to help them secure employment of their own to cover their school fees. Although some of them have succeeded in these endeavors (see next section), most reported feeling frustrated by not having enough money to continue to Form 5 or to attend another kind of postsecondary education program, such as vocational training in hotel management, computers, or small business administration. The following excerpts illustrate some of the most common sub-themes in the essays under the rubric of sponsorship for schooling:

> *Marco:* The last event is my delay to join Form 5. As may be noted, I was in Form 3 in 1996 when we parted. This means I finished Form 4 in 1997 and should have joined Form 5 in 1998 and completed Form 6 in 2000. Due to the school fee problem, however, I failed to join Form 5 in time but did so in 1999.

> *Wilson:* The greatest and only significant problem that I have faced in my life since I parted with you, your husband Timothy, and your child in 1996 is an economic one. I started my secondary education at Njema but when I went to Form 3 I just did it for one term. My parents, due to their poor financial situation, couldn't pay for my fees to enable me to continue with the second term. I had to stay at home for the whole term. Luckily, God helped out and the situation changed. I went back to school and repeated Form 3 but in a different school....I am now in Form 4 and hope to finish school this year.

Unlike the male respondents, few of the young women whose schooling was interrupted after completing Form 4 have since returned to school. Most of them explained this situation by discussing their lack of financial support from their fathers or from sponsors:

> *Lydia*: It [the most significant event] is the loss of my mother's friend who had promised to pay school fees for me....This was indeed a great blow for me because I had put all my hopes in her to help me. I will never forget this death throughout my life.

> *Jeneth*: When I completed Form 4 in 1998, I wasn't lucky to be able to continue with further studies, and my parents could not afford to pay for my upper-secondary education [Forms 5 and 6]. I then tried to ask for help among my relatives, most of whom are also poor. Luckily, my uncle volunteered to pay for me for the first stage of my secretarial course. At present, I am in Dar with my uncle....Life is really tough, and we have no alternative except begging for help from relatives and friends.

Employment and Idleness

The problems of school sponsorship and school fees described in the majority of the essays were often linked discursively to the themes of employment and idleness. In their essays, these secondary school graduates described the ways that gender relations shape employment and educational opportunities, and the conditions under which these opportunities are sometimes procured. The issue of gender relations was more pronounced in the essays that dealt with jobs and training programs because the young women and men have had very different opportunities during these first few postsecondary years. For example, approximately 50% of the young men were still in school; 40% were employed, and about 10% reported being "idle" at their parents' homes. In contrast, roughly 30% of the young women were in school; 30% were employed, and about 40% described themselves as "idle."

There are several explanations for the gender differences in postsecondary school activities that one can discern in the essays, and almost all of them revolve around paternal support for employment and further education. There is a widespread sentiment among these young people that it is very difficult for Form 4 graduates—male and female—to find employment; however, as noted above, young men often have an easier time obtaining jobs and further education because of the financial assistance they receive from their fathers. Although the theme of economic hardship was also evident in many of the young men's essays, they often related it to their own struggles in getting a job whereas the young women's essays usually discussed economic problems in terms of their fathers' inability to help them with postsecondary schooling or employment:

> *Joseph*: Another issue is employment. Here in Tanzania, it's hard for a Form 4 leaver to be hired for a job. Self-employment, such as running a business or agriculture, is the only alternative.

> *Richard*: My father opened a grocery for me, but it went bankrupt. He took it away from me and sold it. My father started a second-hand clothes business, which I still run, but the capital is very small.

> *Jasper*: In 1996, after I completed Form 4, I could not continue with further studies due to my parents' poor financial ability at that time. So I simply remained at home helping them in various activities such as farming, raising animals, and other domestic chores....In 1999 my father got money and sent me to school to continue with high school education that will last up to 2001. At present I am in Form 6.

The young men's essays suggest that fathers frequently help their sons establish themselves in business or aid them in getting a postsecondary education, even when financial difficulties require a temporary interruption in schooling. The young women, in contrast, have generally received less support for education and employment from their fathers in the years following Form 4, although slightly less than 30% are engaged in some kind of postsecondary schooling. The differences in postsecondary employment and education may be the result of a lack of enthusiasm for girls' higher education among fathers and other family members, or these divergent paths might be a consequence of the girls' fathers (and mothers) having lower levels of education than the parents of the male students. Under conditions of *maisha magumu*, people with less schooling may be at greater risk of losing their jobs and experiencing a reduction in household income from other sources, making it difficult to send their children to school:

> *Rachel*: The first major event that happened to me was when my father was retrenched from his job following the privatization of the industry he had been working in. This shocked me deeply because I was still studying at Njema Secondary School and I needed school fees. I contemplated about the school fees, knowing well that I might be

forced to discontinue my studies because there was no other source from which I could get my school fees. But thanks to God we are farmers and had some corn in reserve. So it was sold and I managed to finish Form 4. I did well in my examination and qualified for Form 5, but my parents had no financial ability to educate me further. I tried to send an application for help to one of the organizations [NGOs] in Dar es Salaam, but it wasn't successful. When schools opened, there still was no money. So my father ran to different places borrowing money from here and there so I could go to Form 5 with my colleagues. He managed to get 100,000 shillings that he had to return later. I was very happy to go to Form 5 although I know the problem will recur when I go to Form 6.

Other young women's essays discussed the economic difficulties faced by their fathers and mothers and the consequences of "idleness":

Edina: I personally would very much like to continue with education, but unfortunately my family has no financial ability to enable me do so. My father has no job that gives him income. He is a mason who goes around seeking to repair wall cracks. It's only when he gets one [a job] that he gets some money. But once he gets the money he drinks it all away. In addition, we live in a rental house. In short, my parents live a very difficult life and apart from that they are old.

Martha: Honestly, Dr. Frances, I ask you to look for a way to help me to achieve at least a higher education. I think you know how tempting it is for a youth to stay idle. I have tried to join various groups to run away from such temptations. For example, I have joined the choir group and also learnt sewing.

Lightness: Six months after being idle at home, my cousin came and took me to work in Arusha, where he had just opened a hotel. I stayed in his hotel, where he hired me for a very low salary. From the meager pay, however, I saved a little money and bought myself a bed and a mattress and rented a room because he really mistreated me while I stayed at his hotel.

In these essays, "idleness" is a more complex word than might be expected, referring not only to joblessness, as mentioned by Lightness, but also to a state of increased sexual temptation, as noted by Martha. Some of the young men linked idleness to sexuality in their essays, too, such as in a lengthy paragraph by one former student who was motivated to get a job to "avoid staying idle and falling into youth-prone temptations." This young man was fortunate to have relatives who helped him find a job at a Tanzanian newspaper, but for many others employment cannot offset the "temptations" to which youth are prone.

Sexual Risk

The connection between idleness and sexuality made by some of these former secondary school students reflects a common perception about the health benefits of schooling and other forms of labor. Setel, for instance, illustrates through excerpts from interviews with Chagga youth how hard work is associated with a decline in sexual temptation, or desire (*tamaa*). He quotes a young man who said that "[w]ork tires you out. If it tires you out, you can't have *tamaa*" (1999, p. 163). Desire was alluded to in several of the essays in this study, too, but these young people emphasized the interconnections between sexuality and sexual risk, especially the risk of pregnancy and AIDS.

Table 6: Data on Contraceptive Use from the 2000 Questionnaire

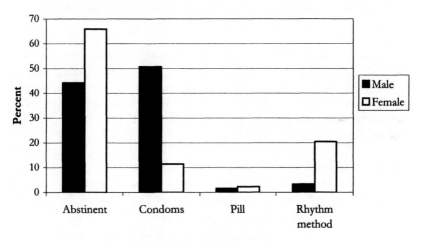

Methods Used With Partners

The data on contraceptive use from the 2000 questionnaire show that many of these young people are sexually active but are not regularly using condoms. Table 6 highlights the significant gender differences between the methods used with partners, with men more likely to use condoms and women more likely to use the pill or the rhythm method. Approximately half of the respondents report that they are still abstinent, but the sexually active youth—especially the young women—are not using condoms to protect against pregnancy and sexually transmitted diseases.

In the essays written by these students in 1996, pregnancy and AIDS were mentioned as problems facing Tanzanian youth in the abstract but seldom as serious concerns for these young people themselves. In contrast, the essays four years later describe personal struggles with these issues as the respondents and their friends cope with unplanned pregnancies and AIDS. This change is probably a consequence of sexual maturity among these young women and men and the worsening AIDS epidemic in the country:

> *Anna:* A lot of events have taken place during the past four years. A lot of deaths of friends and relatives have occurred. Many friends have died of diseases and others from accidents. Some got pregnant while still in school. The events that happened to me are many. First, there was the problem of getting school fees, and I was suspended from time to time. During this time I also met a lot of young men whose major goal was to destroy my life. I, however, managed to deal with them tactfully until I completed my studies.

> *Adella:* Unfortunately, or fortunately, I got pregnant and my parents had to take care of me until I delivered a baby boy who was named —. My parents helped me until the child was seven months old. The child is now nine months old, and after my husband and I decided to start a new life, we both take care of the child. Our life is a very difficult one. We don't know where to get the money from, and we don't know what to do with the child (to help him survive).

> *Vincent:* I encountered serious personal problems in 1999 and in 2000. I did all I could to use contraceptives but in vain. I impregnated two different girls at different times and had to incur all the expenses involved in both abortions. Although they were successful, this was a real big blow and a big lesson to me.

> *Mary:* I would like to speak a little about question 13 [from the survey, see Table 6], which I didn't answer. It's not that I have never had sex but that I have never used any of the methods that are mentioned in that question. This year I haven't played [had] sex at all, and even last year I had sex about twice only. The cause for abstaining from sex is that I am afraid of getting pregnant and also of contracting AIDS and other venereal diseases.

> *Felix:* A sad event is that I lost my most beloved friend and neighbor with whom I was often together. He died this month, July. He wasn't sick for a long time, and it's said he was suffering from AIDS. This is a proof that a lot of us, Tanzanian youths and in Africa in general, will perish if we don't change our sexual habits.

Rose: Among the major events that have happened to me during these four years is my beloved friend and fellow student got pregnant and so got married. She got pregnant while still a student and had to stop her studies. This is why a large percentage of Tanzanian women are uneducated or don't hold public offices—a factor that leads us to be mistreated....Boys don't have this problem because: 1) it is not easy for them to be discovered because girls are afraid to say who impregnated them; and 2) many men prefer running around with female students because they believe such girls are pure and safe from AIDS....Next time I'll give you a more detailed explanation.

Conclusions

The essays by Rose, Vincent, and the others highlight some of the factors that influence the educational, economic, and reproductive health trajectories of Tanzanian youth today. Although this group of secondary school graduates has some important advantages over the majority of young people in the country, many of them are unable to satisfy their desires for more schooling or for formal employment. Moreover, they frequently engage in high-risk sexual behavior even though Tanzanians who have completed secondary school have the greatest knowledge of AIDS of any segment of the population (Bureau of Statistics Tanzania and Macro International Inc., 1997). These examples raise questions about the figure of the "feminist modern" in population and development discourses, the empowered young woman whose education makes her more knowledgeable about sexual risk and better able to encourage the use of condoms with her partners (Greene, 1999).

The conventional wisdom, which I do not dispute, is that adolescent girls from poor households are at great risk for contracting HIV because they often rely on sexual relationships for their survival and have "little leverage around issues such as safe sex and condom use" (Gage, 2000, p. 187). The young women whose views were presented here are not, in general, from the poorest households in Tanzania; indeed, I suspect that my longitudinal research in Old Moshi will show that these female graduates will have lower rates of HIV infection in 10 years than their less-educated counterparts because their sense of themselves as 'educated persons' keeps them from engaging openly in prostitution and encourages them to turn to the church and other institutions to help them avoid "temptations," as Martha put it above. However, the information in this chapter suggests that the "education vaccine" has painful side effects for

some young women who have been inoculated in secondary school (Vandemoortele, 2000, p. 17). For instance, the low sense of self-esteem among many,
though not all, of the young women who reported being "idle" after graduation
is similar to the findings from Serpell's research in Zambia, from which he con-
cludes that rural primary schools "are in the business of producing failures"
(1993, p. 10). One of the reasons for this, according to Serpell, is that the vast
majority of students cannot continue to secondary school because they fail the
national exam at the end of Standard 7, and they have difficulty finding employment because they were taught few practical skills during their primary education.

A similar phenomenon is taking place among secondary school graduates in
Old Moshi: By Form 4, most female students have a strong identity as educated
women, and they imagine a certain kind of life for themselves that, if not obtained, can lead to feelings of failure. Engaging in high-risk sex may simply be a
risk that some of them are willing to take if it provides a step towards this future. Indeed, the students in the 2001 focus groups spoke about the common
view that getting AIDS is like having a car accident: It's common; it's painful; it
can kill you outright, but no one is going to start walking to town, especially not
secondary school graduates.

Despite historical economic and educational opportunities, Kilimanjaro's relative prosperity has not protected its inhabitants from the negative effects of
national structural adjustment programs or from the global AIDS epidemic.
The growth of the informal sector in response to the declines in real wages and
the falling value of agricultural products, such as coffee, have created conditions
of mobility that bring young people into productive and reproductive networks
that often transcend local boundaries and put them at risk of contracting and
spreading the disease. Among youths who have completed secondary school
but desire more schooling, the feeling of being a burden on one's family may
create a willingness to move, even if it means being "mistreated," in Lightness's
words. To be sure, living with one's parents does not prevent a young person
from engaging in high-risk sex, but high mobility, coupled with an uncertain
future, is certainly no prophylaxis.

For youths who cannot find employment after secondary school, the informal
sector provides an alternative to living with one's parents without an income.
Working in the informal economy is not, in and of itself, a problem: Some
women earn more braiding hair and selling pastries on the street than they
would as wage laborers (Tripp, 1997). But these are not the kinds of jobs that

'educated persons' like Mary, Felix, or Lydia have in mind when they say they are looking for work. They imagine a future for themselves that is different from those who have finished only primary school, and employment, in their view, is supposed to reflect those differences. Yet there are simply not enough suitable jobs for all of the secondary school graduates who want them, and therein lies a condition of sexual risk that education alone cannot redress.

The relationship between income deficiency and immunodeficiency is not immutable. [4] However, there needs to be greater attention paid to their interplay today to make sense of the cases examined in this chapter. In so doing, there ought to be a concomitant examination of the *education-as-panacea* concept that does not explain why relatively well-educated young women and men are still taking sexual risks. These recommendations concur, in general, with Farmer's advice: "Arguing, for example, that 'education is the only vaccine' is neither accurate nor wise: since we cannot show that cognitive interventions have been highly effective in preventing HIV infection among the poor—the global risk group—it is surely unwise to rely *exclusively* on such methods" (1999, p. xxiii; emphasis in original).

The epidemiology of AIDS and the political economy of Tanzania are both critical forces in the creation of sexual risk among the poorest *and* among secondary school graduates. Even though it is not possible to change national and global conditions immediately, they can be altered through the policy reforms discussed in Chapter 6 that would lead to a greater commitment to global economic justice. Of course, macroeconomic policy is not, by itself, responsible for the rapid spread of HIV/AIDS in Tanzania and elsewhere, but the rise in consumer prices, the decline in real wages, the imposition of user fees for health services, and the steady increase in school fees over the past fifteen years have made the situation worse, creating a set of conditions under which the virus and the disease can thrive. Changing these conditions would not prevent unwanted pregnancies or unprotected sex in all cases because high-risk behavior is bound to persist in spite of economic reform and more effective AIDS education. Yet policy has a place in combating the epidemic by helping to alleviate the material circumstances that place certain groups of people at greater risk of contracting the disease than others. As we will see in the next chapter, however, many of the policies adopted as part of the structural adjustment framework are instead intensifying, rather than ameliorating, the conditions of *maisha magumu*.

NOTES

1. Setel notes the use of the same idiom about AIDS being an accident at work (*Ukimwi ni ajali kazini*) in his research in Kilimanjaro during the early 1990s (1999, pp. 163–165). Secondary school graduates in other focus groups in my study also used this idiom and often attributed the "accident" to knowing about AIDS but being too drunk or overcome with desire to put one's safe sex knowledge into practice.

2. Stromquist (1999) provides an insightful comparative analysis of the impact of SAPs on gender relations and women's lives in Africa and Latin America.

3. The source of information for Mainland Tanzania and the Kilimanjaro Region is the *Tanzania Demographic and Health Survey 1996* (Bureau of Statistics Tanzania and Macro International Inc., 1997).

4. This play on words comes from the chapter by Setel entitled "The 'Acquired Income Deficiency Syndrome'" (1999).

Chapter 5

"The Water Is Ours": Commodities, Community, and Environmental Conservation

People need to be made aware that water is no longer a free good. It is a finite resource with supply constraints; it has a scarcity value, and there is a cost to using it.
— Narendra P. Sharma et al. of the World Bank, 1996

Rural citizens as well as those in urban areas have to be involved in planning, implementing, running, and incurring the cost for water services.
— Tanzanian Minister of Water and Livestock Development, 2001

If they [government officials] come and install the pipes and check on them, then it's fine to put in meters. But now it is our wives who are going up to the springs because we don't have water from the pipes. What is the meter for? The water is ours; it is ours.
— Bonde focus group, June 5, 2001

The World Bank, the Tanzanian government, and people in Old Moshi are well aware of the critical role of water in improving agricultural productivity and maintaining human health. Are they, however, equally cognizant of the connection between water and schooling? This chapter takes a look at this unexpected pairing in order to show how factors that may seem unrelated to schooling are in fact linked to it in crucial ways—particularly for the poor and the near-poor. For people living on or near the margins, anything that makes life more difficult can push schooling further out of reach. In a community largely dependent upon agriculture, scarce or expensive water can do exactly that. Water can have the indirect effects of cutting into enrollment and attendance, of blunting the power of schooling, in other words, before that power has had a chance to work. If we want to more fully understand what schooling can and cannot accomplish in the Third World, then we have to appreciate more fully the relevance of something as unrelated as water.

Although water is not a unique factor contributing to poverty in Old Moshi, it is uniquely important to this community for several reasons. First, clan-based furrow societies have long played an important role in insuring an adequate supply of water to irrigate Chagga *kihamba* land, where coffee, bananas, and other crops are grown. Since independence, the social significance of these societies has declined, and furrow maintenance has suffered. As a result, it is difficult for people in certain villages to get enough water to irrigate their crops.

Second, the government is proposing to expand its water metering program to include more communities like Old Moshi. Yet many residents fear that this program will have negative effects on those who are most dependent upon free water at public taps for their domestic water needs. Furthermore, as noted in the epigraphs, the World Bank and the Tanzanian government want to make sure that rural residents understand the "cost" and "scarcity value" of water; villagers, in contrast, do not understand how they could be charged for a natural resource that they believe already belongs to them. "It is ours," they argue, and its transformation into a commodity will, they think, only compound *maisha magumu* for the poorest families on the mountain.

Third, the glacier atop Mount Kilimanjaro that supplies water for the Kilimanjaro Region and beyond is melting rapidly, and some scientists predict that it will disappear completely within the next two decades (Gough, 2002; Intergovernmental Panel on Climate Change, 1998; Nash, 2001). Residents of Old Moshi are deeply concerned about this prediction and wonder about their prospects for the future. If "water is life" (*maji ni uhai*), as the Swahili proverb goes, what life lies ahead without adequate water to sustain it? The pages that follow address this question and these three critical concerns about water, poverty, and, ultimately, schooling.

Furrows and Farming During the Colonial Era

It was not only the snow-capped peak of Mount Kilimanjaro that intrigued 19th century European travelers but also the complex irrigation system the Chagga had developed. Hans Meyer, the German who first reached the summit of the mountain in 1887, admired the hard work that went into the digging of the furrows: "The fable that in tropical lands the natives have nothing to do but sit under the trees and let the ripe fruits drop into their mouths could not have originated in Jagga [Chagga land on Mount Kilimanjaro]" (1891, p. 104). According to Meyer, the reason for the Chaggas' hard work, despite their "comparatively backward stage of civilisation" (p. 103), was the irrigation system that allowed them to cultivate food crops and tobacco throughout the year. The abundant water and fertile soil in the area led Meyer to recommend to the German government that coffee, tea, and other commercial crops be introduced in the northern highlands dominated by the Chagga.

The origin of a particular furrow was usually located in the forest zone, far above the inhabited area on the mountain (Moore, 1986). J. R. Currey, a British Agricultural Officer, noted that the digging of furrows "involved the expenditure of immense work and ingenuity." He contended that irrigation was not the primary motive behind the system because the area was blessed by adequate rainfall. Instead, Currey hypothesized that it would "save the women from the hazards of wild animals and from enemies when they were drawing water in the thickly forested river gorges" (n. date).

Regardless of the initial reason for digging furrows, they became very important ways to provide water year-round for crops grown on *kihamba* land. The rights to a furrow usually lay with the descendents of its founder, who were responsible for organizing people to repair the furrow at the end of the rainy season (Moore, 1986). Those who did not help maintain the furrow were obliged to provide large quantities of locally brewed beer (*mbege*) or risk being prohibited from using the furrow in the future. However, as Johnston noted in his 1946 report on land tenure and the *kihamba* system, "it is remarkable that, with a big and complicated furrow system in the kihamba land, so well are matters run by the furrow elders that the number of cases arising out of disputes over water rights are exceedingly few" (n. page).

In Old Moshi, the Muo furrow, which continues to supply water to many of the families in Miti village, has a long and noteworthy history. The chiefdom bordering Old Moshi to the west, Mbokomu, was known as a place where many skilled builders of furrows resided (Stahl, 1964). One of these builders belonged to the Foya clan, an important lineage in Mbokomu along with the Maanga and Mrema clans (Stahl, 1964). According to Ramos Makindara, the late son of the last chief of Old Moshi, Jacob Foya moved from Mbokomu to Old Moshi seeking protection from the chief, and he extended the Muo canal from one chiefdom to the other (personal communication, 10 June 2001).[1] The British colonial account, however, explained that "this most historic furrow," critical to the water supply of Old Moshi, had "in generations past been the cause of wars and was taken from Mbokom [sic] by Mandara" (Superintendent of Education, 4 July, 1928). By either account, the presence of this productive furrow was one of the arguments used by colonial officials fond of Old Moshi to advocate for building the government Central School for boys at this site rather than in western Kilimanjaro (see Chapter 2).

The furrow system continued to interest Europeans, especially as settlers and colonial administrators sought greater control over sources of water on the mountain. The British administration temporarily banned the building of new furrows in 1923 due to water problems European farmers were having on the plains below, but this policy did not last long because officials recognized that irrigation was crucial for Chagga farmers on Kilimanjaro. However, by the middle of the 1930s, the colonial government was quite concerned that water was being wasted through faulty furrow construction, so they began projects to improve the furrows and their catchment areas (Grove, 1993). Johnston's report suggested that it was the intensification of agriculture on the mountain that had led to "careless irrigation and erosion." He recommended that the government prohibit "irrigated mbege" (finger millet) because he saw this crop, or perhaps the local *mbege* beer itself, as the primary source of environmental problems (1946). Another colonial report on agriculture in Kilimanjaro, written after World War II, stated that even though "soil conservation measures have been enforced by Native Authorities for the past ten years," the development of farms in the plains below the main tarmac road "will require Government control in order to secure the best use of the available irrigation waters" (*Native agriculture*, n. page).

Commercial agriculture, especially with Europeans farming the plains, was becoming an environmental concern for the government. So, too, was the worsening shortage of *kihamba* land due to population growth, a shortage that officials feared might lead to political unrest. For example, Johnston argued, "The Chagga tribe is continuing to increase rapidly and the Chagga are naturally extremely land-conscious and rightly fear the coming status of landless men. Just as the enclosures in sixteenth century England produced a similar unhappy class of landless men so will the Chagga of the near future suffer, landless, unless a long-term far-sighted policy is adopted now" (1946, n. page).

A Far-Sighted Policy? Postcolonial Water and Agriculture Programs

After independence, many of the colonial government's catchment area improvement programs were abandoned because the new government had other priorities. In particular, the Nyerere administration was concerned with developing a centralized socialist state, and it therefore eliminated the chiefdom system on Mount Kilimanjaro. This political change resulted in the gradual decline of clan-based systems of governance, such as the furrow societies, in some communities on the mountain (Grove, 1993).

The new administration also sought ways to meet the needs of the majority in ways that fit with the rural development philosophy of *ujamaa*. In the agriculture sector, the government provided subsidized agricultural inputs (e.g., fertilizers, pesticides, and seeds) and extension services to smallholder farmers, especially in *ujamaa* villages (World Bank, 1994). Agricultural businesses, such as import/export companies, food processing factories, and plantations, were nationalized, and guaranteed prices for certain crops were established through a pan-territorial pricing system (World Bank, 2000). The Nyerere government also regulated the market for many food crops within Tanzania through cooperative organizations to which farmers sold their crops; commercial sales were prohibited. In addition, the government subsidized the price of certain food items—maize flour, for example—as a further sign of its commitment to covering the basic needs of the population (Ponte, 1998).

In the water sector, the government made "Free Water for All" one of its development goals because it recognized that many rural households could not pay to improve the water supply in their locale (World Bank, 1999). Beginning in the late 1960s, "water became a free good for a rural dweller" because the Nyerere administration covered costs for capital investment and recurrent expenses (Maganga et al., 2002, p. 922). In 1971, a new policy stated that the government would provide safe water at convenient public facilities for all rural residents within twenty years (Therkildsen, 1988). From 1971 to 1980, the proportion of Tanzanians with improved, if not entirely safe, water increased from 12 to 47 percent (World Bank, 1999).

Although the Nyerere government was officially following a socialist path to development, this did not mean that it eschewed the advice of the World Bank. On the contrary, the Bank prepared a report in 1961, the year of independence, which stressed the importance of government investment in the country's irrigation networks and in developing an agricultural credit program for farmers.

However, in the 1970s, the Bank's recommendations to the Tanzanian government began to change, and by the mid-1980s its advice was to "liberalize" the pricing and marketing of foodstuffs and export crops, and to "restructure" government parastatals in the agricultural sector (World Bank, 1994, p. 171).

Since the beginning of structural adjustment in the mid-1980s, Tanzanian policy and World Bank recommendations for the agriculture and water sectors have grown ever more similar. This is not surprising considering that most agricultural loans come from either the World Bank or the International Fund for Agricultural Development in Rome (Cooksey, 2003). Nonetheless, the discursive convergence warrants examination because it illustrates the concept of developmentalism very well. For example, in keeping with the advice of the Bank, Tanzanian agricultural policy "has advocated a gradual shift towards private sector ownership of commercial enterprises, and the use of market determined prices and incentives in the agriculture sector" (World Bank, 1994, p. xxiii). More specifically, these changes include the elimination of subsidies for fertilizers (Cooksey, 2003), the promotion of hybrid seeds and agricultural technologies, and the reduction of agricultural import restrictions (World Bank, 1994). The assumption underlying these reforms, according to the Bank, is that in order for agricultural productivity to increase, "subsistence farmers need to be brought into a market economy where the availability of consumer goods provides incentives for cash generation and off-farm sales" (1994, p. xvi).

The water sector has also undergone a profound restructuring as the *ujamaa* era of state-centered development has given way to the current period of market-driven development. In 1991, for example, the Tanzanian Parliament approved a new water policy that included a number of changes, including the introduction of user fees and the development of a local water management program (Maganga et al., 2002). Since then, the country's two most important river basins, the Rufiji and the Pangani (which includes the Kilimanjaro Region), have become the focus of a World Bank-funded program called the River Basin Management and Smallholder Irrigation Improvement project (World Bank, 1996). Illustrating its current support for both public and private involvement in development (see Chapter 1), the Bank intends for this project both to "strengthen the Government's capacity to manage water resources and address water related environmental concerns," and to "improve stakeholder participation in basin management and irrigation scheme operation" (p. 15).

Two more recent documents further illustrate the changes that have occurred in the water sector during the past decade: the 2000 *Poverty Reduction and Rural*

Water Supply draft policy (RWS) published by the Tanzanian Ministry of Water (United Republic of Tanzania, 2000), and a 2001 speech given by the Minister of Water and Livestock Development during a meeting of Parliament in Dodoma, the capital of Tanzania (United Republic of Tanzania, 2001a). The RWS policy gives priority to private involvement in water service provision and management and to cost-sharing programs at the local level. It also calls for greater community participation to achieve its objectives because the role of the state is limited to providing knowledge and advice as "a facilitator, regulator, and promoter of rural and urban water supply and sewerage services" (p. 16). The principal strategies and actions for the rural water sector are as follows:

> (a) Promoting community participation and cost sharing in rural water supply activities; (b) Maintaining, rehabilitating water schemes and securing of new capital investment; (c) Promoting the use of appropriate technology; (d) Encouraging private enterprise to develop and intensify privatization; (e) Enhancing human resource development; (f) Developing water sources for urban and rural areas; (g) Improving efficiency in the sector; (h) Improving the environmental sustainability of water supplies; (i) Promoting conservation measures and proper management of water resources; (j) Undertaking institutional reform, evolving new organisational structures, enhancing capacity and promoting decentralisation; and (k) Reviewing the regulatory and legal framework. (pp. 8–10)[2]

A similar set of strategies is described in the minister's speech to Parliament. In it, he highlights the role of the private sector and of the community in providing water services. The minister begins by outlining a number of steps being taken to improve water resources through projects financed by NGOs and by the governments of Japan, Germany, and the Netherlands. Of particular relevance to the case of Old Moshi, as we will see below, is the promotion of village water committees as part of the overall "decentralization policy" (in English) whereby "projects should begin at the bottom with the citizens instead of at the top levels of the government" (translated from Swahili, p. 6). The participation of citizens is emphasized later in the speech when the minister describes future directions for improving the rural water supply with the assistance of the World Bank. Again, the appropriate procedure for rural water projects is described—in English—as a "bottom up approach and demand responsive approach." Continuing in Swahili, the minister states that "The Ministry will encourage the private sector to participate, especially in running projects on behalf of the citizens or the government" (pp. 13–14).

The close relationship between the World Bank and the Tanzanian government means that 'Tanzanian' policies in a number of sectors increasingly converge with the recommendations of the World Bank (Vavrus, forthcoming). This convergence is particularly clear in the water sector, where privatization and community participation in service provision are consistently advanced. For example, the Tanzanian minister notes in his speech that the current national water policy "realizes that water supply is not a social service alone but an economic service as well" (2001a, p. 6; translated from Swahili). This is strikingly similar to the language in the Bank's *African Water Resources* report noted in the chapter epigraph: "People need to be made aware that water is no longer a free good. It is a finite resource with supply constraints; it has a scarcity value, and there is a cost to using it" (Sharma, 1996, p. 27). Instead of the government stepping in to make the water system more efficient, as in colonial policy, the current recommendation of some government officials and international financial institutions is to use the market—that is, higher costs—to motivate conservation among putatively wasteful farmers.

Recalling the discussion of neoliberalism in Chapter 1, it appears that this economic perspective is driving current water policy in Tanzania. Water, as with other environmental resources, needs to be viewed as a commodity by the people who use it or else, so the argument goes, it will be wasted. As Jacobs writes of this view, "If the environment is *not* treated like a commodity, society will allocate it 'sub-optimally'—protecting it too little (less than people are willing to pay for its benefits) or too much (more than they are prepared to pay). In general, the environment exhibits 'market failure'" (1994, p. 75; emphasis in original). Yet this perspective, popular as it may be among policy makers, ignores the possibility that people consider water and other natural resources to be public goods critical to the social welfare of their community (Rees, 2001). Moreover, water often has social-symbolic significance, as in Old Moshi, that makes it unlike commodities that people buy and sell for personal gain (Mosgrove, 1998). The next section shows that these matters of social welfare and symbolic significance complicate the inter/national market model of water conservation.

Water and Agriculture Policies on the Ground

Some of the shortcomings of the neoliberal perspective on environmental conservation became clear to me on one of my first trips to Tanzania. While on an extended stay in Dar es Salaam during the dry months of September-November of 1992, I had many conversations with neighbors about the water problems we were experiencing on the periphery of the city. I, too, recall my own frustration on this first encounter with urban water shortages in Tanzania. We awoke many mornings to find no water coming from the tap, and our only recourse was to ask our neighbors if we could draw water from the private storage tank they had built. Feeling rather uncomfortable about turning to the same family so often, I began to inquire about how other people were getting water. I found that most people—rather, most women and children—were waiting in line with large plastic buckets to take their turn at the water tanks that were irregularly delivered to the neighborhood. Women would fill their 5-gallon buckets and then hoist them onto their heads, and their young children would follow suit by filling their small plastic bottles and carrying them back home.

The care that I observed, and learned to practice, when washing dishes, clothes, and body during this dry spell in Dar raised many questions for me about the urban residents who were often blamed in the government press for the water problems we were experiencing. The broken water pipes and the diversion of water for industrial purposes received less attention in the newspapers than did the careless citizens who needed to be educated about conservation. Yet inadequate environmental education hardly seemed to be the main problem; it was the lack of funding to upgrade the water system that called out for government attention.

Over the next decade, I saw similar scenes of women and children carefully carrying water from public stands to their homes, especially in rural communities. In a country where only 2% of rural residents have piped water in their homes, people have learned to use water with care because it is a labor-intensive task to collect it each day (Bureau of Statistics Tanzania and Macro International Inc., 1997). Thus, without treating water as a commodity that is bought and sold, most people recognize that there is a cost—a labor cost—to using it. And more education about water conservation is unlikely to make rural residents much more efficient than they already are.

Water and Social Welfare

As I learned more about the geographic differences in Old Moshi, I realized that it was rare for people on the eastern side of the Msangachi Valley to have piped water in their homes even though it was quite common among my neighbors in Miti on the western side of the valley. I began to wonder whether such differences in resources might be correlated with school enrollment, so Mr. Moshi and I included questions about water in the survey we administered to children and their parents in 2000 (see Introduction).

The survey was designed to identify the factors that might explain who goes to secondary school after completing Standard 7. When we began in 2000, all of the children were in Standards 6 or 7 at four of Old Moshi's 11 primary schools. In the summer of 2001, we conducted a follow-up survey to find out which children enrolled in Standard 7 in 2000 had started Form 1 the following year. We also held focus group discussions with parents to talk about the results of the 2000 survey, including the open-ended questions where parents often mentioned water and agriculture in relation to schooling. We began with focus groups in Bonde and Mbali villages, on the eastern side of the valley.

The slippery mud from the early morning rain made the walk down into the valley quite treacherous for someone like me, unaccustomed as I was to trekking along the winding paths while the clay on my boots grew heavier with each step. "This is *really* the path that everyone takes to get from Miti to Bonde each day?" I asked Mr. Moshi, as he gracefully stepped from one stone to another across the river that divides the more prosperous western side of Old Moshi from the less prosperous eastern edge of the community. There are many students, teachers, and day laborers who walk along this path from Bonde to Miti and back each day, usually in search of schools or jobs better than the ones available closer to home. I had an inkling of the economic differences between the two sides of the valley from my household survey in 1996, which revealed greater access to electricity and piped water on the western side of the valley compared to the eastern side. At the time, Mr. Moshi explained that the difference was due primarily to the well-used road that traverses the western ridge and connects at the southern end to the tarmac road leading into Moshi Town. However, the road was not located on the western ridge by accident. Historical factors have given this area near Chief Rindi's former home many advantages; the road manifested those advantages even as it added to them (see Chapter 2). And now, five years after our first household survey, we were able to present the results of a much more comprehensive study that showed striking differences in socioeconomic resources on the two sides of the valley.

The 2000 survey contained questions about household composition, resources, and educational attainment for each member of the Standard 6 and 7 students' families. In every category, the families whose children attended Mbali Primary School, located furthest north on the eastern ridge of the valley, had the fewest resources, and their children performed most poorly in school. The other school village on the eastern ridge, Bonde Primary School, also had lower levels of resources than the two villages on the western ridge. For example, few families in Mbali and Bonde had electricity or piped water in the home, and they were far more dependent upon public taps to obtain water for domestic and irrigation purposes. Moreover, it was only in Mbali and Bonde that a significant number of families reported regularly having inadequate food to eat. Table 7 summarizes the results of this portion of the survey.

Table 7: Socioeconomic Profile of
Four Primary School Communities, 2000

Primary School	Children ever born	Electricity in home	Piped water in home	Public water tap: domestic purposes	Public water tap: irrigation purposes	Inadequate food to eat
Sokoni	5.0	77%	62%	27%	31%	2%
Miti	5.9	46%	56%	10%	9%	0%
Bonde	6.3	10%	25%	63%	44%	12%
Mbali	6.3	2%	17%	64%	56%	32%

The information about education in the four villages is more complicated because socioeconomic level did not always correspond to children's performance in school. For example, Table 8 shows the expected pattern of greatest household spending on schooling in the wealthiest village—Sokoni—and lowest spending in Mbali, the poorest village. However, parents in Bonde spent the same amount on education as parents in Miti even though Bonde is, on average, a less prosperous village. It was also in Bonde that children scored the highest on the numeracy test that was a part of the survey they completed in 2000; in contrast, children in Miti scored the highest on the reading comprehension test that provided a rough measure of their literacy skills. During focus group discussions, parents and teachers in Bonde explained that the anomalous results on the numeracy test were due to the math teachers' hard work at Bonde Primary that compensated for more limited resources in their pupils' homes. During discussions in Miti, parents suggested that the school's proximity to Njema Secondary School, with its long and distinguished history in northern Tanzania, may have created in Miti an educational climate richer than that in other communities in Old Moshi.

Table 8: Educational Profile of
Four Primary School Communities, 2000–2001

Primary School	Women with post-primary ed.	Men with post-primary ed.	House-hold spend-ing on ed. per child	Mean numer-acy score (4=high-est)	Mean lit-eracy score (4 = high-est)	Std. 7 grads who started Form 1 in 2001
Sokoni	8%	56%	28,054 ($33)	2.17	2.06	83%
Miti	20%	49%	13,751 ($16)	2.29	2.32	60%
Bonde	11%	43%	13,889 ($16)	2.40	1.98	49%
Mbali	10%	0%	7,562 ($9)	1.46	1.79	30%

The final column in Table 8 shows the percentage of Standard 7 students who began Form 1 upon completing primary school. Given the high cost of secondary schooling today, it is not surprising that children from the wealthiest villages were the ones most likely to continue in school. The difference between Sokoni, where over 80% of the children started Form 1, and Mbali, with a mere 30% matriculating, shows that the great disparities in this community are reflected in school enrollment patterns.[3] It should be noted that, as a group, girls continued to Form 1 at a slightly higher rate than boys, even though the correlation between being female and continuing in school was not statistically significant.

The question of who starts secondary school is central to this longitudinal study, so we conducted further analysis to see which variables from the survey had a significant effect on the odds of a child beginning Form 1. First, we considered two-dimensional relationships and found that a number of variables had a significant effect (at the .05 level) for both male and female students. These included high level of schooling for parents as well as a number of indicators of relative affluence: hired help on the family farm, electricity, piped water, a television, or a house made out of cement. In general, these results suggest that children whose parents have high levels of education and the most resources are more likely to continue to Form 1. There were other strong relationships revealed in the analysis that did not quite reach the .05 significance level, such as the link between having a high class rank in Standard 7 and starting Form 1.

After looking at different variables, we evaluated the simultaneous effects of several of them on the probability that a Standard 7 student would start Form 1. We selected variables for our logit model based on the univariate analysis, i.e., we included those variables that we knew had a significant effect or a strong relationship with students' continuing to Form 1. The variables with significant positive effects—meaning significant positive coefficient estimates—were high class rank in Standard 7, high parental level of education, small *kihamba*, and hired help on the family farm. The variables with significant negative effects on the probability of starting Form 1 were insufficient food in the household and selling large quantities of coffee. These findings suggest that families in Old Moshi that are most dependent on the sale of coffee for their livelihood but are unable to hire agricultural laborers are less likely to have children who continue in school to the secondary level. We found that such families are located disproportionately in Mbali.

Despite the differences in socioeconomic resources among the four school villages, the people who attended the focus group discussions in 2001 voiced nearly identical concerns about how environmental changes and policy 'reforms' in the water and agricultural sectors were undermining social welfare throughout Old Moshi. They recognized the political-economic constraints that limit the very possibility of a quality education and of a better life for poorer residents of the community, but this recognition had not diminished their faith in schooling to solve development-related problems. At Mbali Primary School, for example, parents were strongly in favor of higher education for their children, even though their daughters and sons have the lowest odds of continuing to secondary school. One father explained:

> In fact, we parents would really like our children to get a higher education. However, you find that a child is quite intelligent, but when the students do their final [Standard 7] exam, you hear that she was not one of the ones selected for Form 1, or sometimes only two children are selected because the school was unable to prepare the children to pass the exam....So you just don't understand what the government is thinking, especially for schools like ours in remote places. There are very few children who pass the exam, as opposed to schools in town where many children may pass. Another thing is the issue of school fees. In fact, school fees hurt parents like us a lot. This is because in Tanzania right now there are no employment opportunities. Many people are at home,

they have no jobs, and yet the government raises taxes with the other hand. So you find that you cannot buy your child clothes or do anything because you have no job. Therefore, poverty increases day after day. (Mbali focus group, June 11, 2001)

Upon further discussion, it became clear that these "taxes" were in fact the rising costs of the inputs that farmers like this father need to grow coffee and maize, inputs which the government no longer subsidizes. According to people in all of the focus groups, the most problematic of these inputs is artificial fertilizer, which farmers require because there are no longer enough cattle in Old Moshi to produce manure for all the farmers in the community. The price of hybrid seeds and pesticides, also considered essential items for farming today, make farming more costly than in the past. Moreover, the interdependency of chemical fertilizer and hybrid seeds means that if one wants the higher yield of 'foreign' seeds, then one must use fertilizer.[4] In response to my question about whether chemical fertilizers were used when the participants were children, one man quickly interjected: "No, in the past we did not use [chemical] fertilizer. There were indigenous seeds (*mbegu ya kichagga*; Chagga seeds), but now they've brought us these hybrid seeds sold in shops, like 51/50 or 41/41 developed in Malawi. If you don't use fertilizer, you get absolutely nothing because the land has lost its fertility" (Miti focus group, June 6, 2001).

Such criticisms of chemical fertilizer, pesticides, and hybrid seeds do not mean that farmers longed for the days of manure and hand hoes. Indeed, the focus groups and the open-ended questions on the survey about farming past and present showed that people have generally embraced these new technologies; nonetheless, they find farming difficult because the small amount of *kihamba* land available to most families means that high yields, and thus costly inputs, are essential. When we began talking about problems related to farming in the past, one older woman at Mbali spoke passionately about her past labor: "There were no tractors to do the ploughing of the land as there are now! In addition, there were no means of transportation, and we used our heads to carry our crops home. Now we are using motor vehicles" (focus group, June 11, 2001). However, an elderly gentleman asked to give his contrary opinion:

Teacher, I would like to contribute a little about the past and now. Farming in the past! There were very few people then! The population was very small, and people were not destroying the environment. There were big forests and at the water sources there were big ponds or dams that could be filled with water even though the technology then was quite limited. A person could farm with hand hoes and would get a few crops....Now we have vehicles that till the land. We have insecticides/pesticides to apply to the crops, but farming has become difficult because of our own action of interfering with the water sources, of cutting down the forest. There is no more water, so although we use modern technology when farming, we fail to get good results....There is modern technology, but we have destroyed the environment. (Mbali focus group, June 11, 2001)

The ambiguity surrounding fertilizers and motorized vehicles is evident here. On the one hand, women have long been the ones responsible for hauling bananas and other foodstuffs from home to market, and a pick-up truck makes this task less arduous, to say the least.[5] On the other hand, more vehicles mean more trees are cut down to clear paths wide enough for people to drive from the main road to their homes, which are usually set back from the road on their *kihamba* land. According to people in all the focus groups, the loss of trees means a decline in soil fertility and a greater dependence upon chemical fertilizers, whose use, it was often noted, is linked to health risks like cancer.

In these narratives, it was clear that individuals' actions are linked to community welfare. People blamed themselves and their neighbors for the environmental problems in Old Moshi rather than outside forces, and they repeatedly said that "we" are the ones who must work to improve the situation. Although people were nostalgic in many instances about the abundant forests and fertile soil of the past, there was no concomitant rejection of 'modern' agricultural practices. There were some older people like the man above who idealized the past, or parts of it, but there were an equal number whose memories of the hardships of bygone days made them glad they were gone. Much like the farmers described in Gupta's work in India, the people in Old Moshi embrace many of the intensive farming practices advocated by the World Bank and the government while simultaneously critiquing those practices, especially their negative effects on soil fertility and on people's health (1998). However, on one matter—the furrow societies—people were in agreement that past practices were superior to present ones. The next section explores some of the differences between local views on these societies and inter/national perspectives on community participation in water management.

The Social-Symbolic Significance of Water

A few months before returning to Old Moshi in 2001, I heard a report on the radio about a research team at The Ohio State University predicting that the ice cap atop Mount Kilimanjaro would disappear within the next twenty years. Initially, I was rather skeptical because the intrepid Hans Meyer had made the same claim after his three ascents of Kibo peak between 1887 and 1896 (Geilinger, 1936). However, after lengthy discussion about global warming and tropical glaciers with my brother-cum-climatologist, Steve Vavrus, and after reading some of the articles to which he directed me (e.g., Higgens, 2001; Intergovernmental Panel on Climate Change, 1998), I began to appreciate the potential local consequences of global environmental change for people in Old Moshi. And I knew that this would be a topic worthy of discussion during the focus groups even though its relationship to schooling was indirect.

When I arrived in Moshi, one of my first stops was at the regional administrative office building to discuss my research permit. On the bulletin board in the main lobby were two articles from Tanzanian newspapers, with one bearing the headline "Doomsday for Kilimanjaro people in sight" (Ngatara, 2001). "Scientists from the United States of America have recently come up with a verdict that the famous snows on the top of Mount Kilimanjaro will completely vanish within a period of less than two decades," read the first paragraph. The reporter went on to criticize the government for its pumping of water from the mountain down to urban areas. "This is done while the rural Kilimanjaro dwellers who are the rightful owners of the water go thirsty and unwashed most of the time," the author maintained. The story concluded that while scientists may believe that global warming is the cause for the melting snow, people on Kilimanjaro feel it is due to their neglect of traditional religious practices as more and more people have converted to Christianity and Islam: "Is it any wonder now when Ruwa (God) of the people of Kilimanjaro seems to have been completely disgusted by the ways of His people and as during Noah's era is determined to destroy them by drying up 'Mother Kipoo' [Kibo peak] their source of livelihood?" Intrigued by this article, not to mention its prominent spot in a government office building, Mr. Moshi and I decided to speak with someone in the regional water department to get an official view on the story of the melting snow and on water resources in the Kilimanjaro Region.

The Deputy Regional Water Engineer for Kilimanjaro welcomed us and spent a good deal of time discussing the possibility of the melting ice cap and the policies that are being implemented to conserve water. Although this official had heard about the Ohio State study, he was skeptical about the conclusions the researchers had drawn because he thought their analysis was based only on measurements conducted during the dry season, when the glacier always retreats. The far greater concerns, he argued, were deforestation and the "misuse" of water through wastage. The water engineer told us that there is a national tree-planting campaign that provides trees to people in rural communities but that the problem in Kilimanjaro is that "community participation is low." The current policy to combat deforestation and water wastage works "from the bottom upwards," meaning that local committees are being formed to enforce rules against the planting of crops within 300 meters of a natural water source and to make sure that leaking pipes at public water taps are fixed promptly.

The topic that generated the most discussion, however, was the important role the water engineer saw for village water committees because of the planned expansion throughout Kilimanjaro of a water metering system currently in operation in Rombo (eastern Kilimanjaro) and Hai (western Kilimanjaro).[6] First, he described how each village is supposed to have an elected water committee responsible for reporting waste, such as broken pipes and leaky faucets at public water taps, to government officials. For the Hai project, the Tanzanian government has received funds from the German Development Bank to help establish a metering system in which "every point in this scheme"—that is, both public and private taps—is metered to promote water conservation. In Rombo, 300,000 people are involved in a program where houses are metered for their water use or, if no meter is used, a flat fee of 900 shillings per month is charged. Even though charging a flat fee may not encourage conservation to the same extent as metering, it is, according the water engineer, supposed to cultivate an understanding that water is a commodity that is not to be wasted.

The water engineer's enthusiasm for the metering system and for the community water management program was infectious, so I temporarily accepted his assessment and tried to put aside my academic concerns that these 'Tanzanian' plans closely resembled World Bank recommendations for other Third World countries with very different histories (Pitman, 2002; Sharma et al., 1996). I continued to wonder, however, if these community participation and metering programs were, in fact, local responses to specific environmental problems in Kilimanjaro. Or were they responses manufactured elsewhere and then 'sold' to officials in Kilimanjaro in the hopes that they would look 'Tanzanian' to local community members? To what extent, I wondered, was either the problem (water waste) or the solution (community policing of this 'crisis') genuinely local? The water engineer gave us a chance to explore these issues by asking whether we would add two questions to the list of topics for our focus group discussions to help him gauge (1) local awareness of the water committees, and (2) interest in the metering system in Old Moshi. I agreed, never realizing that these queries would evoke the strongest reaction of all the topics we discussed.

There were mixed responses to the first question from the water engineer about whether people were aware of any elected water committees in Old Moshi. In all of the focus groups, at least one person could name a member of the water committee, but it was evident that the committees were not well known, and their duties were unclear to most people. For example, at Miti Primary School several people shook their heads to indicate that they had never heard of such a committee.

> *Woman:* I know the water committee exists, but I don't know what it does.
>
> *Man:* They are new committees, and they are committees in theory but not in practice.
>
> *Woman:* They are more active in private than in public.
>
> *Man:* They are there only to be shown to any *NGOs—sponsors*—who might come around, but they are very inactive.
>
> *Woman:* They don't do anything.
>
> *Man:* They just pretend to do work, but they're cheating about work. No one knows them. It's a government effort, but they're just shadows. (Miti focus group, June 8, 2001)

The second question, about the proposed metering system, elicited strong negative reactions among almost all of the participants. Although there were a few people who agreed that the metering plan might make people more conscious of their water use, the general reaction was not merely opposition to the plan but outrage that those to whom this natural resource belongs should now be forced to pay for it. It was clear that people did not see water as a commodity like sugar or flour that one purchases each month. In contrast, they felt they had 'paid' for water through their labor: They had dug the trenches and laid the pipes themselves without much government assistance. Moreover, people were concerned about the social welfare aspect of the metering proposal because of its impact on the poorest families, who might not be able to pay for water and would end up with none at all. Written excerpts from the focus groups can only partially capture the dismay and disbelief over the proposed commodification of water in Old Moshi:

> If they put in meters and I don't have money, it will be a great problem for us. They need to compare the rich, who can afford meters, to the poor who cannot. For example, this woman [pointing to his right] needs water but has children and no husband. Where will she get the money? When they come to read the meter, they will want money and where will she get it? How to solve this problem? They have to compare those with means and those without. (Miti focus group, June 6, 2001)

> Let me explain further, it's like this: For the water that is purchased in town, there is no one who goes to dig a trench for the pipe or does anything! The water user enters a house and finds the water and a meter. If they use a lot or a little, it is up to them. It is different for citizens here in this village, where we organize ourselves to go and do this work, to bring this water with our own sweat. We have dug deep, until we have un-earthed human leg bones at depths of five to six feet.... It's not the property of the government or the water department. It's the people's. They only assisted in giving the pipes. Now then you tell me that meters are going to be installed at the standpipes. For example, this pipe [points outside] that is being used by the school students? [general laughter]. When such pipes get damaged, we provide our own labor and repair them to avoid the wastage of water. There is no government that comes to do this job for us. (Mbali focus group, June 11, 2001)

> The government doesn't have the right to charge us for water because we dug the fur-rows, and when we have a problem, the government is not there to solve it. During the dry season, you may not have water for a week. The government should do more re-search to find out people's water problems before installing meters. (Miti focus group, June 8, 2001)

In contrast to the suspicions surrounding the elected water committees and the discontent with the metering plan, there was a general desire among focus group participants to revive the furrow societies as a way to reduce dependency on piped water for irrigation. As shown in Table 7, most of the villages—Miti being an exception—rely on piped water for irrigation because the furrows have fallen into disrepair. The focus groups at Miti and Mbali had the most detailed discussions of the furrow system because in these two areas, higher up the mountain, the furrow societies were once most active. For each furrow mentioned, people could identify the clan associated with it and the current leader.[7] The leader, or chairman, is the person who coordinates the annual cleaning and repair of the furrow, organizes the water allocation schedule and punishes people who break the rules of the furrow association (Gillingham, 1999). The chairman is also the person who leads people to the intake of the furrow because his presence is believed to help insure that the water will flow properly (personal communication, E. Matee, August 17, 2002).[8]

The "most historic furrow" described in colonial records, the Muo canal, was the one people most frequently cited when asked to describe the traditional furrow organization. "Ka Foya" (Foya's place) was the other name for the Muo canal because it was begun by Jacob Foya. Confirming the colonial account of tensions between Mbokomu and Old Moshi, people in the focus groups explained that Chief Abraham of Old Moshi took control of the furrow from the Foya clan, and as a result, the water disappeared. "I don't know exactly what makes these things happen," noted one person in Bonde, while another added, "It's the spirits, the ancestors of the Foya clan" (focus group, June 5, 2001). Others described how certain prayers and offerings to the clan ancestors, along with the cutting of a symbolic tree branch, are necessary to insure that the water flows well each year: "The clan is responsible for fulfilling customary prayers to the ancestors of that particular clan. When people go to work on the furrow, they must go with the clan leader. Before working on the furrow, the clan leader must pray and then he cuts something [a branch of a certain tree] to signify the beginning of the work. The clan leader does this first and then work can begin" (Miti focus group, June 8, 2001). When people do not adhere to these practices, people said that there would be problems with the water supply just as one finds today.

Who Owns the Water?

The furrow societies in Old Moshi may or may not be revitalized in the years to come, but it is likely that the metering system will be implemented because it has the support of prominent financial institutions and government officials. Because people with electricity in their homes are accustomed to being charged for metered usage, why is there such strong opposition to paying for water in the same way? The primary reason seems to be the belief among Old Moshi residents that they have already paid for water through their labor, and they are not keen on committees—elected or not—collecting money from them when they have little to spare. "The water is ours," argued one older man in Bonde, and thus charging for it simply made no sense to him.

These sentiments, expressed in slightly different ways at each of the focus groups, appear to be shared by people in other parts of the Third World whose lives are connected through global water privatization policies. The case of Bolivia is illustrative because water privatization has gone much further there than in Tanzania, and people's opposition to this development program has led to violent street protests. With World Bank support, private companies have become involved in the provision of water to urban and rural communities. One problem private companies encountered in La Paz, the capital, is that in some poor neighborhoods people were simply not using enough water for the company to make a profit. The reason is that the residents, mainly Indians who had developed their water conservation habits in the Andean countryside, "were extremely careful with water, never wasting a drop, and they continued to be so even after they had taps installed in their homes" (Finnegan, 2002, p. 53).

Meanwhile, in the rural Bolivian community of Villa San Miguel, a water cooperative was formed in 1994, and residents helped to dig the well that was financed in part through Danish aid. In 1999, the government privatized water systems in the area, including this well, and sold it to a private consortium. The new water law that is a part of national privatization policies in Bolivia allows companies to put meters on wells and charge people for their water. Similar to the reactions in Old Moshi to the very thought of meters on facilities built by the people themselves, residents in this Bolivian community began to protest, sparking a "water war" in which government troops were brought in and organizers arrested (Finnegan, 2002). It is not difficult to imagine similar forms and levels of resistance in Kilimanjaro should the metering system go into effect. As one man in Bonde village suggested: "If they [the government] put in meters, people may destroy them" (focus group, June 5, 2001). This destruction would not only represent anger toward privatization policies in general but also at the commodification of water, a substance that most people view as 'theirs' as a community and not for sale.

Conclusions

This chapter has examined one of the factors making it difficult for some people in Old Moshi to send their children to secondary school: water. "Water is life," the Swahili proverb goes, and thus it affects far more than agriculture and health. Although there is no necessary connection between water and schooling, I used this meaningful pairing for people in Kilimanjaro to show that education exists in a vast web of social and political-economic relations. It alone cannot transform people's lives, in spite of policy makers' talk about *education as panacea*. If parents, like those in Mbali, cannot afford piped water in their homes or do not have adequate water to irrigate their crops, then it is unlikely that they will be able to pay for secondary schooling for their children. In communities where making a living off the land is increasingly difficult, as in Old Moshi, access to water and affordable agricultural inputs are critical *education* issues even though they may not appear to be so at first glance.

One of the stated objectives of the World Bank and the Ministry of Water and Livestock Development is to reduce poverty and improve health conditions among the most vulnerable groups in rural communities. If this is indeed the goal, then it seems unlikely that the water metering plan as currently envisioned is going to achieve it. People may actively protest such a policy, or it may simply end up quietly harming the poorest households even further. Resentment of this policy stems from its neoliberal assumptions about how the market can best allocate environmental resources when, in fact, social welfare goals and social-symbolic factors affect people's values and preferences about water. As Jacobs argues, "The debate is really about the social and moral structure of society. Should more and more decisions, even ones about public goods, be left to markets, devoid of wider moral consideration? Or should some be retained within the sphere of political institutions, subject to the interests of the 'public good'?" (1994, p. 81).

The next chapter explores several local efforts to promote "the public good" in the areas of environmental conservation, HIV/AIDS prevention, and job creation for primary school leavers. These NGOs clearly consider moral issues to be integral to their development work even if those issues may, at times, be at odds with the priorities of donors. The organizations also demonstrate how 'local' solutions to development problems can be both sensitive to the specific historical circumstances of a community and attentive to the "globally and nationally circulating discourses of development" (Gupta, 1998, p. 6).

NOTES

1. Stahl (1964) names Paulo Foya as the founder of the canal, but interviews with several prominent members of the Old Moshi and Mbokomu communities—including the great-grandson of Paulo Foya—suggest that the canal was started by Paulo's father, Jacob.

2. The RWS lists a number of more detailed solutions under each of these strategies, but I have listed only the heading for each strategy because of space limitations.

3. It should be recalled that only 6% of the population attends secondary school (based on the net enrollment ratio), so the figures for all of the villages in Old Moshi are still much higher than the national average (National Bureau of Statistics, 2000).

4. See Gupta (1998, chapter 4) for similar views on themes discussed in the remainder of this chapter, including chemical fertilizers, hybrid seeds, and water resources.

5. See Moore (1986, p. 25) for an interesting pair of photographs showing Chagga women in 1902 and 1973 transporting grass for their cattle on their heads. Although there was general agreement in 2000 in Old Moshi that the number of stalled cattle was inadequate today to provide manure for all who needed it, women are still seen each day along the main road carrying fodder by the head load to their animals.

6. Mosgrove (1998) provides a fascinating socio-historical account of changes in the irrigation system in western Kilimanjaro. He, too, notes the shift from the "social partnership" that supported the furrow system to the monetary relationship with water that current policies encourage (p. 176).

7. The most often cited furrows in the focus group discussions were Chemchem, Huyank-ambo, Kiserecha, Komanjoro, Kwa Mbere, Maktiha, Menyeri, Ngalachu, and Seremengi.

8. Mr. Matee is a senior member of the community and a relative of the Makindara family.

Chapter 6

Postcolonial Interventions in Education, AIDS, and the Environment

In this book, I have examined an enduring development concept—*education as panacea*—through a case study situated in an analysis of the broader social and political-economic contexts that affect schooling in Tanzania today. Even though Old Moshi may not be typical of the rest of the country, it does provide an instructive setting in which to explore the enduring impact of colonialism, developmentalism, and global capitalism on everyday life. For instance, the educational disparities that arose during the colonial period linger into the present; one finds the highest concentration of secondary schools in regions that had the most mission and colonial schools, such as Arusha, Iringa, and Kilimanjaro (see Table 3, Chapter 2). Developmentalism also continues to be an important force in Old Moshi and elsewhere as development organizations expand their scope across the country. With the Tanzanian government seeking more and more help from national and international organizations, the power of these organizations to define the country's problems will only increase. Local NGOs, so often underfunded, may find it tempting to focus on these problems, perhaps at the expense of more pressing local ones if doing so will mean support from the larger organization. Finally, global capitalism largely determines local commodity prices, from coffee grown in Bukoba and Moshi to tobacco in Songea and Tabora. When market prices tumble, so, too, do enrollment rates and medical care in families that depend on cash crops for their livelihoods.

The worldwide expansion of schooling during the past four decades has provided children in Africa with far more opportunities to obtain a basic education than existed during the colonial era. However, from the early 1980s to the late 1990s, the net primary school enrollment ratio declined in several African countries, such as Tanzania and neighboring Kenya (World Bank, 2001). In addition, fewer high school and college students in these countries and others find formal employment after graduation because there are more graduates and fewer civil service jobs than there were a few decades ago. Despite these problems, faith in schooling continues unabated among many groups, including youths in Old Moshi, their parents and kin, policymakers at the Tanzanian Ministry of Education and Culture, and officials at the World Bank.

This book has shown that the instrumental value of schooling to foster development pales in comparison to its ideational importance. I have argued that the abiding desire for schooling at the local, national, and international levels is not because it *causes* fertility decline, safe sex, or environmental conservation per se; instead, schooling fuels the imagination of individuals in relation to a group of proximate or distant others with whom one shares an affinity (Appadurai, 1996; Boym, 2001). For students at Njema Secondary School, their sense of belonging to a community of 'educated persons' means that they will strive to have no more than four children; this restraint will show that they have the knowledge necessary to cope with *maisha magumu*. In a similar way, development planners in Dar es Salaam and Washington, D.C., live thousands of miles apart but still belong to the "relatively small, interlocked network of experts" that design and implement policy in Africa (Ferguson, 1994, p. 258). To be an expert today means to foreground certain assumptions about development, and promoting women's schooling is one of the most potent examples of this expertise.

Exploring the postcolonial condition in Old Moshi, marked by the tripartite features of colonialism, developmentalism, and global capitalism, has been my way of connecting local lives to national and global contexts. I have attempted to do justice to Gupta's contention about case studies and the postcolonial condition: "To examine a particular site carefully... is not to do a 'local' project" (1998, p. 337). With this maxim in mind, I have engaged in different levels of analysis to show how the problems in this particular setting are related to broader discourses of developmentalism and to material inequalities heightened by global capitalism. In addition, I have engaged with different material than one typically finds in a book about schooling to debunk the belief that education—both formal and non-formal—is sufficient to transform entrenched social and political-economic disparities around the world.

This process of debunking began in Chapter 1 with an examination of the trope of the "feminist modern" in international development policies (Greene, 1999, p. 227). I argued that the empowered, educated woman in these texts is a welcome contrast to earlier representations of the oppressed Third World woman (Mohanty, 1991); nonetheless, I explained why it is problematic, to say the least, to place the onus of national development largely on one group—women—and on one institution—the school.

The second chapter shifted the focus from international policy to local practice by examining changes in the social and political-economic context in which schooling occurred during the 20th century in Tanzania. Through this discussion of colonial and postcolonial policies, I showed how schooling—especially for girls—has been considered a cure for, or a cause of, development problems at different points in time.

In Chapter 3, I examined more closely the culture-as-cure concept in relation to sex education for secondary school students in Old Moshi. Using material from classroom observations and interviews, I illustrated the difficulty of developing culturally appropriate curricula when students, teachers, school officials, and church leaders differ in their interpretation of Chagga culture. The anti-family planning views that Njema students encountered on campus raise questions about how directly schooling affects or can affect fertility decline.

These questions remained in Chapter 4, where I looked at the views of secondary school graduates regarding condom use and sexual risk in an era of AIDS. The inverse correlation between years spent in school and HIV infection suggests that there is an "education vaccine" for women (Vandemoortele, 2000, p. 17); however, as in the previous chapter, it is unclear how schooling could be inoculating against the disease when AIDS education and/or information about condoms is absent from the curriculum. Furthermore, I argued that even though health education is obviously a crucial first step in reducing HIV transmission, it is not a panacea for slowing the spread of AIDS when economic decline is coupled with a strong desire for further schooling.

Chapter 5 moved from the school grounds to the fertile land upon which many Chagga families make their living. Taking up the culture-as-cause argument, I explored the proposed water privatization program to promote conservation in Old Moshi. I used multiple sources of data—archival records, interviews, observations, and surveys—to challenge the assumption that new forms of community participation and governance are needed to control local farmers' profligate environmental practices. I also looked at changes in the viability of small-scale coffee and maize production and showed that families with the greatest dependence on agriculture were the least likely to have children who matriculated to secondary school. Mbali, the village farthest from the main roads, continues to experience the most severe deprivations of *maisha magumu*, including the lack of resources to improve its primary school and to pay for more children's secondary schooling. Nonetheless, parents in this village, like their counterparts elsewhere in Old Moshi, have a strong commitment to schooling.

Were it not for friends in Moshi and Manhattan, I might have concluded the book with the summary above rather than the section that follows about interventions in the areas of education, HIV/AIDS, and the environment. Patient and supportive when reading drafts of the previous chapters, my colleagues nonetheless pressed me to explain how this book might contribute to the transformation of developmentalism and the international policies about education derived from it. I was uneasy with this assignment because it could result in yet another "cookie-cutter approach" to policy formulation that applies the same strategies for change to all countries (Adelman, 2001, p. 118). However, my discomfort was assuaged by rereading the Epilogue to *The Anti-Politics Machine*, wherein Ferguson articulates his response to questions about what should be done to alleviate the problems that development organizations seek to redress:

> If the question 'what should they do' is not intelligibly posed of the government, another move is to ask if the 'they' to be addressed should not be instead 'the people'....But once again, the question is befuddled by a false unity. 'The people' are not an undifferentiated mass. Rich and poor, women and men, city dwellers and villagers, workers and dependants, old and young; all confront different problems and devise different strategies for dealing with them. There is not one question—'what is to be done'—but hundreds....It seems, at the least, presumptuous to offer prescriptions here. The toiling miners and the abandoned old women know the tactics proper to their situations far better than any expert does. Indeed, the only general answer to the question, 'What should they do?' is: 'They are doing it!' (1994, p. 281)

The diversity of people devising strategies to combat social and political-economic problems in Kilimanjaro illustrates that there are, indeed, many tasks to be done and many different tactics to accomplish them. Yet the postcolonial condition in the region means that there is no strategy of 'the people' unaffected by 'the expert.' Tanzanians who have started NGOs often use technology developed by American or European engineers as in the cases of the Qoheleth Foundation and the Tanzania Environmental Action Association described below. Or they may ask foreigners with skills in accounting to assist in the establishment of loan schemes (e.g., the Mkombozi Vocational Training Centre), or they might approach people with expertise in counseling to teach members how to work with families affected by HIV/AIDS (e.g., KIWAK-

KUKI). Local NGOs may also need foreign financial assistance to initiate or, in some cases, to sustain projects that cost more than members can fund themselves. These circumstances can, and often do, perpetuate the top-down, donor-driven model of development that tends to offer the same solutions to disparate problems.

The four NGOs discussed in this chapter are not immune from the problems scholars have identified for other voluntary associations, such as insufficient accountability to their constituencies, oligarchic governance by group leaders, or incorporation by the state (Edwards & Hulme, 1998; Fisher, 1997; Kamat, 2002). Moreover, these NGOs are not a panacea for the education, health, and environmental dilemmas facing many people in the Kilimanjaro Region today. Combating such complex problems as HIV/AIDS and deforestation will take far more bilateral and multilateral aid, including expertise, than most countries—the United States, in particular—are currently willing to contribute.[1] Addressing the political economy of international development will also require restructuring aspects of national policy in the First World, such as the agricultural subsidy programs for American farmers that make it difficult for non-subsidized farmers in the Third World to compete in global markets (Kristof, 2002). These are the macro-level dimensions of development that local NGOs can barely begin to address.

Despite the limited impact of local NGOs on international policy, the examples that follow illustrate the important contributions they can make in the lives of individuals in their communities. I refer to their activities as postcolonial interventions because they bring together 'the people' and 'the expert' in ways that were impossible during the colonial era, when power relations were profoundly unequal. In addition, these organizations challenge the strand of developmentalism that represents African women as "ignorant, poor, uneducated, tradition-bound, domestic, family-oriented, victimized, etc." (Mohanty, 1991, p. 56). Finally, they each confront local hardships that are compounded by the downturn in coffee prices on global commodity markets and by the vagaries of the job market as state-owned companies are privatized and their workforces downsized by their new owners.

Each of the Tanzanian NGOs discussed in this chapter emerged from local concerns and utilizes locally appropriate tactics; however, they are unabashed about their relationships with foreign experts and international donors because they see these connections as beneficial rather than detrimental to the long-term viability of the organization. I have gotten to know these groups over the years as I have sought to become more involved in addressing the major problems discussed in the book, namely, education, youth unemployment, HIV/AIDS, and environmental degradation. In selecting these four organizations, I seek to draw attention to their efforts—limited as they may be in the larger scheme of things—but I do not hold them up as exemplars to be modeled indiscriminately by groups in other countries.[2] They represent the diversity of approaches to development in this locale, and they are undoubtedly "doing good" for most of the individuals with whom they work (Fisher, 1997, p. 439). However, they cannot take the place of a sustained international development program that operates through governmental *and* non-governmental institutions.

Interventions in Kilimanjaro

During the *ujamaa* years, the Tanzanian government incorporated a wide variety of civil society groups into its fold. Therefore, a mere 17 non-governmental organizations were registered by the state between independence in 1961 and 1978. However, the economic crisis of the late 1970s and early 1980s made NGOs more attractive to the government, and their numbers began to climb steadily. By the mid-1990s, there were more than 800 registered NGOs, and the current figure is in the thousands (Kelsall, 2001; United Republic of Tanzania, 2001b). In the Kilimanjaro Region, there are NGOs addressing education reform, health care, human rights, and environmental conservation. There are also several umbrella organizations, such the Union of Moshi Rural Non-Governmental Organisations (UMRU-NGO), that bring together different groups for joint planning and action. Formed in 2001, UMRU-NGO seeks to coordinate rural development activities in the area that includes Old Moshi:

> UMRU-NGO, as an umbrella NGO, aims to create a forum where NGOs/CBOs [community-based organizations], Local Government, private sector, civil society and any other stakeholder can meet and jointly chart out future plans of action, so that they can effectively and efficiently play the role as catalytic agents for change and take up their roles as equal and active partners in [sic] development process. (UMRU-NGO, 2001, p. 2)

The first group I will discuss, the Qoheleth Foundation, was formed in 1996 with 17 members and a director and became a registered NGO in 1998. It seeks to promote youth and women's development in rural areas of Tanzania through a wide range of programs. Mr. Muhubiri, the director, is a chemical engineer by profession, but he left his job to start the NGO because of his concerns about the "exodus of youth from rural areas to urban centers" (interview, August 17, 2002). His motivation also stems from his religious convictions; the son of a minister, and a devout Christian himself, he is committed to "doing God's work." His wife, who shares these views, allocates part of her salary from the hospital where she works to pay for the cost of renting a small office for the Foundation.

Since its inception, the NGO has focused on two primary rural development activities: HIV/AIDS education programs and a sustainable development project promoting the use of low-cost building materials. With less than $2,500 contributed from international agencies and individuals for the 1998–2001 period, the Foundation has still managed to carry out many activities that promote an awareness of how youth unemployment is related both to AIDS and to environmental degradation. For instance, it has worked with international and regional NGOs to conduct workshops for in-school and out-of-school youth "to promote youths [sic] awareness of their vulnerability to HIV/AIDS" and "to promote youths [sic] friendly STDs/HIV/AIDS-counseling services and voluntary HIV blood testing services" (Qoheleth, 2002).

In the area of sustainable development, the Foundation has embarked on an education and training program to demonstrate that stabilized soil blocks provide a viable alternative to local timber in the building of schools and homes. In the Rombo District of eastern Kilimanjaro, where soil erosion and deforestation are serious problems, the NGO has established a project at a secondary school to teach students and out-of-school youth to produce the low-cost blocks by combining cement and soil. They have completed a two-room canteen at the school that serves as a demonstration house for the community. The Foundation has also finished two houses in Moshi using its Action Block Press machines, showing urban residents that the blocks are strong enough for home construction. These houses serve another function as well: They have been built for low-income relatives of children whose parents have died of AIDS as an incentive for extended families to care for children orphaned by the disease. "In the past, children were considered to be everyone's children, and any adult would care for them," Mr. Muhubiri contends (interview, August 17, 2002). Today, however, poverty and AIDS itself have increased the pressure on poor families, and they often need help to care for these AIDS orphans. Mr. Muhubiri's long-term goal for the Qoheleth Foundation is to become self-sustaining through the sale of stabilized soil blocks produced by youth who might otherwise be unemployed.

Figure 4: Mr. Muhubiri (left) Demonstrating the Action Block Press to Mr. Moshi (right)

Sharing the goal of sustainability is Mrs. Mshana, a former home economics teacher who started the Mkombozi Vocational Training and Community Centre in a low-income neighborhood in Moshi. The Centre, registered as a community-based organization, opened in 1999 as a place where, according to its brochure, "members work together to cultivate skills toward liberation from all kinds of oppression, social, economic or political towards the creation of positive social change."

An enthusiastic and articulate woman, Mrs. Mshana is deeply involved in co-ordinating four different types of activities. At the Centre itself, there is a technical education program for primary and secondary school graduates as well as short courses for adults. Depending on the program of study, students take classes on such topics as food production and nutrition, tailoring, computer skills, and foreign languages (English, French, and German). A second program at the Centre is the community health education program, which includes programs on HIV/AIDS and maternal and child health taught by area nurses. The Centre also offers classes on broader issues related to children's rights and on legal education that are led by experts from other NGOs.

The third set of activities at the Centre revolves around youth and women's employment. With assistance from a Dutch-Tanzanian NGO, Mrs. Mshana helped to start the Moshi Economic Youth Group that now involves 15 wards in the Moshi Municipality. The Regional Commissioner demonstrated his support for the group by donating 100, 000 shillings (approximately $100) to establish a bank account that the youth can use to attend national youth meetings and to organize events in the Kilimanjaro Region. The Centre also helps to organize a microenterprise program affiliated with the Tanzania Home Economics Association (TAHEA) and a revolving credit program. In 2002, the Kilimanjaro branch of TAHEA opened up a small shop in Moshi where members sell items they produce, such as batik, wood carvings, cheese, and sundried foodstuffs. Similar to Mr. Muhubiri's philosophy, Mrs. Mshana believes that "we are sustainable," even though she recognizes the importance of financial and technical assistance from national and international agencies in reaching this goal (interview, August 15, 2002). One way of working toward self-sufficiency is the TAHEA shop itself. Each woman pays membership fees (about $10 to join and $5 per year to maintain membership), and 5% of each sale is put toward maintenance of the shop. The remaining 95% of the sale, however, goes to the woman who produced the goods.

Finally, there is a rotating credit program for women and men that Mrs. Mshana started when she was still teaching home economics at the Moshi Technical College. Based on a local income-sharing concept (*kibati*), the idea is that all members contribute a specified sum each week, but one member collects all of the funds. Another member is the recipient of the pooled resources the following week, and it continues in this fashion. However, Mrs. Mshana noted that there were problems with this system early on because people were spending the money on domestic needs, such as clothing, rather than investing it in income-generating projects as was intended. Therefore, she found a consultant from the Netherlands to help for a few weeks to set up a bank account, and another foreign volunteer provided guidance for two months while a re-

vised loan program was established. The system now in place involves groups
of five people who each contribute 5,000–10,000 shillings per month. They also
pay 1,000 shillings for pre-membership and pre-loan training. After four
months, a person is eligible for a loan that is twice the size of the entire group's
contribution during that period. When it started in 1995, the maximum loan
was 200,000 shillings (approximately $200), but now it is above 1.5 million (ap-
proximately $1,500) for the 480 members in the program. With a ratio of 8
women to 2 men, Mrs. Mshana hopes that the program will contribute to a
more equitable "gender balance" in the economic activities of the home and of
the community at large (interview, August 15, 2002).

The third NGO, the Kilimanjaro Women's Group Against AIDS (KIWAK-
KUKI), is the oldest and the most widely known outside of Kilimanjaro because of its links with national and international organizations and actors.
Begun in 1990 in Moshi Town, KIWAKKUKI has been described as "unique
in Tanzania as a democratic forum where women of diverse economic, educational, and social backgrounds have joined together to set an agenda for local
AIDS activism" (Setel, 1999, p. 86). Its membership remains female, but men
participate actively as counselors and as honorary members. Although it is difficult to capture the philosophy of the organization, Setel mentions that members
often draw upon the "medico-moral discourse" used by many people involved
with AIDS education in Kilimanjaro (1999, p. 173). For instance, he describes a
speech given by a male Lutheran pastor to conclude a KIWAKKUKI seminar
to train members to visit the homes of people affected by AIDS. Most KI-
WAKKUKI members with whom Setel spoke—both male and female—
approved of the pastor's comments regarding the sexual dangers posed by the
large market outside of town, the ineffectiveness of condoms, and the importance of a Christian life in preventing AIDS (1999, pp. 173–175). Setel notes,
"In Kilimanjaro, AIDS educators have communicated with audiences by mixing
medical information with images of misallocated energy, desire, business, and
the personage of the *mhuni*" (a hooligan or rebel) (1999, p. 172). These images
were similar to the ones I discussed in Chapter 3, where pastors and teachers in
Old Moshi admonished students not to use condoms or birth control pills. I
was curious, therefore, to see how these discourses affected the work of KI-
WAKKUKI in Old Moshi.

To learn about its activities on the mountain, I invited members of two KI-
WAKKUKI branches from different parts of the community to attend a focus
group discussion. The nine people who participated—one man and eight

women—spoke at length about their activities and their goal of expanding their services, especially to support families with children orphaned by AIDS. Both branches have started only in the past three years, but they have grown to include men, such as pastors from area churches and local government officials, as honorary members. The support of churches is especially important because they take up collections periodically to supplement the approximately $100 per year that each branch receives from the regional headquarters. Supportive pastors have also cut short their Sunday sermons to allow time for KIWAKKUKI members to make presentations at church. As one participant put it, "Because there are people who do not want to see [the presentations] ('or even hear them,' shouted another person), they are compelled by the pastor to continue to stay on even though they may not like it" (focus group discussion, August 17, 2002).

The participants' reasons for joining KIWAKKUKI varied. Some spoke of religious convictions, others of their growing awareness of the AIDS problem as nurses and or as neighbors of people with the disease. Several women noted their personal concerns about contracting HIV/AIDS and their desire to learn more about disease prevention. For example, one woman gave the following frank explanation for becoming active in the NGO:

> I joined KIWAKKUKI after I had a patient who was suffering from HIV/AIDS. In fact, I am saying it plainly, I have my co-wife who unfortunately caught this disease. When I heard that there is this KIWAKKUKI group, I thought it was a good idea to join them so that I might learn how to take care of this patient so that I would not get infected. Because if you don't understand these things, for example an HIV/AIDS patient may develop mouth sores and [sores] elsewhere, and if you have not learned anything you can be negligent and you can catch the disease as well. Therefore, it was important for me to join these people to get more training. (focus group discussion, August 17, 2002)

Many of the participants talked about the training they received at the KIWAKKUKI headquarters that has helped them counsel people with AIDS and provide health education lessons at local schools. One of the most important aspects of the counseling is privacy; many AIDS-affected families are not yet ready for their neighbors to know that a KIWAKKUKI member has come to call. Once communication and trust has been established, then the members provide services, from health education to school fees for the children to "the word of God":

•When we go to visit, we go like we are visiting any ordinary patient in our village. But if s/he decides to declare it to us, then we can visit the person as an infected HIV/AIDS patient.

•And in addition, for those who have not gone to the hospital, if you get some time to stay with them you can know their condition. Then they may begin to explain to you how they are getting sick and so on, so using some counseling techniques you begin to probe them about how they would feel about going to get tested for these many diseases, like malaria and others....Others may easily tell you, "Maybe it's HIV/AIDS." Or they may say, "Maybe I have already caught this disease!" And you may reply, 'How do you know? If it's this one, then it's a good idea to take a test'....But another person may just stay and look at you without saying anything. With this one you had better be careful because if you tell him [about the test] in haste, he may decide to kill himself. Another may simply say, "It's God's will," and you cannot oppose it. (focus group discussion, August 17, 2002)

Those members who make presentations in primary and secondary schools say that the problem of AIDS is so large in Tanzania today that they face little or no opposition from school officials when they ask to speak with students. However, they made it clear that the instructional methods they use, such as "inviting experts and conducting video shows," do not include information about condoms:

Even us, when we teach the students, we do not teach them about condoms. We teach them to avoid bad behavior, to change their behavior, and to first know God. Those things [sex] they will encounter much later on, and they are not for now. So when we give education in schools, this is the most important thing that we explain to the children. (focus group discussion, August 17, 2002)

The last broad topic in the focus group concerned the problem of children orphaned by AIDS. KIWAKKUKI headquarters sponsored 21 children in local primary schools, but the participants lamented their inability to do more: to help more of these children and in bigger ways.

Participant: Therefore, when we visit the orphans, we face a great burden. You may find that a woman [who died] left four children and had nothing to help these children. In most circumstances, the children live with difficulties; they get their education with difficulties and even to get a school uniform is difficult. In fact, this issue of orphans is quite big here in our village.

Fran: But who do these children live with?

Participant: They live with a grandmother or aunt or distant sister.

Participant: And here you find a woman may have her own children, but then she is given more to take care of.

Participant: Or other children are taken by any person who may not be related to the family.

Participant: Just any person! (focus group discussion, August 17, 2002)

Echoing the sentiments expressed by Mr. Muhubiri, the members of the Old Moshi branches of KIWAKKUKI are concerned about children orphaned by AIDS, but they know that, with resources so limited, they cannot cover all the costs of the orphans' schooling and medical care.

The final NGO discussed in this chapter, the Tanzania Environmental Action Association (TEACA), shares with the others a modest resource base but a committed membership and a small group of national and international supporters. Its brochure states explicitly that TEACA "is an independent Nongovernmental, Non-religious and Non-political organization" whose objectives are to provide environmental education, to contribute to reforestation efforts, and to help conserve water. TEACA headquarters are located at a primary school in Mbokomu, the former chiefdom that borders Old Moshi to the west, but it has branches in the Arusha Region and in Dar es Salaam as well. Although TEACA receives support from international donors—in particular, the Japanese government and a Japanese environmental organization—it generates much of its income through a variety of microenterprise projects. These include selling seedlings from one of its 10 tree nurseries, selling honey from its 40 beehives, and selling fish from the ponds it created with Japanese assistance. The TEACA branch in Kilimanjaro raises around $800 per year from its nurseries and about $400 from the sale of honey. Because many coffee farmers in the area are facing financial problems, members of TEACA, who have paid the 600 shilling (60 cents) yearly membership fee, can receive a special variety of coffee seedlings that is supposed to resist insects and so reduce the need to purchase pesticides. By selling tree seedlings cheaply and by giving away coffee trees, TEACA aims to benefit the community because, as the founder puts it, "We deal with the grassroots-level people" (interview, August 20, 2002).

One rainy morning in August, Mr. Moshi and I set out for TEACA, hiking up the steep and slippery valley walls that separate Mbokomu from Old Moshi. As we approached the primary school where TEACA is based, we could see that the buildings are well maintained and decorated with attractive maps and posters. Across from the school building stands a cattle stall, and underneath it runs a biogas pipeline. The pipe leads from a deep storage tank under the stall, where the biogas is obtained from cow manure, to two large round earthen stoves in the school kitchen. When the school cooks need to prepare food, they can turn on the gas and use these stoves, or they can cook over a wood-burning stove that has been specially designed to use very little firewood. Near the school kitchen is one of TEACA's tree nurseries, which contains not only a variety of indigenous and foreign tree species but also an innovative "landless farming" demonstration that shows people how to grow certain plants vertically if their *kihamba* is small. For example, cabbage seeds can be inserted into small holes cut into the sides of gunny sacks filled with dirt, and the cabbages will grow to their full size along the sides of the sacks.

When we met up with Mr. Foya, the founder of TEACA, he explained that his motivation for starting the group was his concern about deforestation in this community on the edge of the Kilimanjaro Forest Reserve. He arrived at the primary school in 1986, when he became the headmaster, and he observed that the government was harvesting trees without replacing them. Mr. Foya obtained 1,000 seedlings in 1987 and began replanting them by the nearby river with the help of teachers and other concerned members of the community. Starting as a formal group in 1989 and registered by the state in 1997, TEACA was able to persuade the government to allow members to plant seedlings in bare forest land; the government also agreed not to cut the trees without notifying the group. The group has expanded beyond Mbokomu, but its core members remain the teachers at the primary school. This provides an ideal and also unusual opportunity for Tanzanian teachers to integrate environmental conservation into the curriculum, and this is exactly what is happening at the school. As TEACA members, the staff has learned about reforestation and alternative forms of energy, and some of them bring this knowledge into the classroom in teaching the social studies syllabus for Standard 7. Mr. Foya admitted that the environmental studies component of the syllabus is complicated and "hard to teach," but he and other teachers at the school are attempting to do so for the nearly 300 students at the school (interview, August 20, 2002).

Mr. Moshi and I marveled as Mr. Foya explained in detail each of the environmental conservation projects at the school, but we were perhaps even more surprised to make the historical connection between these contemporary activities and those that had occurred in Mbokomu more than 100 years earlier. Recalling the account of "the most historic furrow" described in the previous chapter, we wondered whether our ingenious host was related to the talented Jacob Foya, who is credited with engineering the sophisticated irrigation system that serves Old Moshi. "Yes," Mr. Foya replied, "he was my great-grandfather." Mr. Foya told us that the Foya clan gathers in Mbokomu every year during the Christmas holiday, and he invited us to join their festivities and to ask the older members of the family my unanswered questions about the history of the furrow. I added this invitation to my growing list of 'future projects,' said my goodbyes, and set off for Old Moshi.

Final Thoughts on an Unfinished Project

These four examples demonstrate, to paraphrase Ferguson (1994), that some Tanzanians are "doing it" quite well without the support of international financial institutions or government agencies, support that might come with many strings attached. However, as with schooling, NGOs are not a panacea for the entrenched development problems facing countries and communities in the Third World. The problems that these NGOs are addressing are local, but they are global as well, and they demand international action to alleviate them over the long term. For instance, it is likely that people in Old Moshi will confront water shortages in the coming decades due to global climate change from industrial activity thousands of miles away. They may also see education and health indicators fall even further if coffee prices on global commodity markets do not stabilize. Local problems are also affected by national policies and priorities in the education and health sectors, which means that the Tanzanian state continues to have an important role to play in the development process even as it seeks ever more private sector involvement in the provision of social services.

The myriad problems that globalization brings to the fore make it difficult to respond to Ferguson's other question in his Epilogue: "What should we do?" (1994, p. 282). Who is the "we" that should do more about education, HIV/AIDS, and environmental degradation? The primary group that Ferguson identifies is also the audience that I am principally addressing, namely, "scholars and intellectuals working in or concerned about the Third World" (1994, p. 283). By witnessing, documenting, and publicizing the local effects of national and international development policies, scholars can draw attention to crises that might otherwise be neglected by politicians and policymakers. Those who are also teachers can bring their research into the classroom to show how local actors are responding to changes triggered by regional and global transformations. Moreover, through sustained engagement with local NGOs, schools, or health programs, scholars can help these groups secure at least some of the technical and financial assistance they need but from outside of the typical development network—from individuals and institutions, in other words, that are less likely to try to dominate the partnership. In short, I am proposing a two-pronged approach for scholars—myself included—who can publicize through their writing and teaching the inequalities of international political-economic relations and the inadequacies of development via NGOs but who nonetheless work with these organizations to foment change, albeit limited, in the here and now.

A second "we" that I have in mind for this book are students who want to apply the lessons learned in their university classes to improve social and political-economic conditions around the world. If the international graduate students I teach are typical of others, then there is tremendous energy and commitment among many people studying international development today. However, the unrelenting critique of developmentalism in our seminars casts a pall over the classroom by the end of the semester. "What can we do?" is the inevitable question. Some of the most thoughtful answers from students include the development of expertise about one country—learning its major language(s) and history and staying abreast of current affairs—and the attempt to bridge the gap between theory and practice. In making these suggestions, students are beginning to imagine a different kind of development, one that promotes depth of understanding over speed of assessment. They are also calling for different ways of combining social theory and empirical research rather than rejecting the former as too abstract or the latter as too applied. In addition, there are many who seek "critical friendship," a phrase that Edwards (1999) uses to describe "a loyal but challenging relationship in which both sides practise what they preach, and each trusts the other to find ways forward which fit their reality best" (p. 226). Developing such a relationship takes time, but there is no better time to begin than during the years when students are beginning to identify themselves as scholars.

Waxing optimistic, I venture a final "we" among the readership of this book: politicians in First World countries and policymakers at international financial institutions. I put these groups together because of their influence over foreign economic assistance, even though I recognize the diversity of views within and between them. If it were possible to unite politicians and policymakers around a common agenda for action, then its two principal items ought to be debt elimination and steep increases in international aid. Stiglitz (2002) provides a more detailed list of reforms than this one, which includes creating better social safety nets, banking regulations, risk management, and responses to international financial crises. Yet he, too, recommends the elimination of debt as a precursor to meaningful change in the process of international development.

I also support Stiglitz's call for an increase in the amount of aid given to Third World countries and an easing of the conditionalities placed on structural adjustment loans (see Chapter 4). He notes:

> Relatively small amounts of money could make enormous differences in promoting health and literacy. In real terms, adjusted for inflation, the amounts of development assistance have actually been declining....There needs to be a basis for funding this assistance (and other global public goods) on a more sustained level, free from the vagaries of domestic politics in the United States or elsewhere. (2002, p. 243)

Several politicians, including British Chancellor Gordon Brown and former Mexican President Ernesto Zedillo, have gone further to suggest a program for the Third World similar to the Marshall Plan that aided postwar Europe ("Brown's 'Marshall Plan,'" 2001). Such an international fund would be administered by the United Nations to help insulate the flow of aid from national politics. Increasing international aid by $50 billion a year as the Zedillo plan recommends would require a dramatic expansion of assistance from many high-income countries, especially the United States. The current political climate makes it unlikely that such a change will be forthcoming; nevertheless—to speak optimistically once again—it is possible that the military path to international engagement will someday be abandoned and a new course chosen, one marked by greatly expanded and sustained federal support of employment and educational programs, comprehensive health services, and environmental conservation projects in the Third World. Such a plan would cost more than the U.S. currently spends on non-military international aid, but it is worth remembering that a mere four decades ago the U.S. was committed to much higher levels of foreign assistance (Shapiro & Birdsall, 2002).

In the years to come, I plan to work toward these policy reforms at the international and national levels. I also intend to remain actively involved with schools and NGOs in Kilimanjaro because there are problems at the local level that require global attention and global problems that only longitudinal case study research can document. Yet as Ferguson points out, there may be little need in the future for the research and advocacy skills that academics like myself are currently trained to use. Instead, he contends that "different kinds of knowledge and skills will be required [and] that the nature of our intellectual activity itself will have to be transformed in order to participate in this way" 1994, p. 287). Although "this way" is left undefined, I take it to mean doing research in a post-colonial way, with the hyphen added intentionally to emphasize the diminution of developmentalism and the cultivation of 'decolonized' relationships that foster collaborative research across continental divides (Mutua & Swadener, forthcoming).

Yet "this way" is about more than changing how research is structured and by whom it is conducted; it is also about the hard physical work that needs to be done, in addition to one's scholarship. This work is modest, incremental, and largely unrecognized by the committees that sanction the labors of students and faculty in academia. It is about raising money for schools that have no textbooks; it is about bringing food and medicine to families affected by HIV/AIDS; it is about digging trenches and planting trees together with the 'subjects' of one's research.

The problems discussed in this book, and many others that might have been, are vast, complex, and intractable. A lifetime of learning about and working on them just might begin to make a difference. Perhaps that is the most useful course: to forget the search for a panacea and to settle in for the long haul.

NOTES

1. The current administration of President George W. Bush boasts of its expansion of foreign
    economic aid but is in fact proposing relatively minor increases, for example, the rise from
    $11.5 billion in 2002 (expressed in 2003 dollars) to $11.6 billion for 2003. When the 2003
    amount is expressed as a percentage of the economy, it is the second lowest level during the
    post-World War II period, at 0.11% of the Gross Domestic Product (GDP) for 2003
    (Shapiro & Birdsall, 2002). This figure can be compared to the larger share of the economy
    that was spent on aid in the 1960s (0.58% for 1962, for instance) and to the much higher
    levels of aid provided by many First World countries. Most high-income members of the
    Organization for Economic Cooperation and Development (OECD), for example, typically
    allocate three times more for foreign economic aid than does the United States (ibid).

2. For readers who want to contact these organizations, they can be reached at the following
    addresses: (1) Qoheleth Foundation Tanzania, P.O. Box 6436, Moshi, Tanzania (or via email
    at qft2000@yahoo.com); (2) Mkombozi Vocational Training Centre, P.O. Box 968, Moshi,
    Tanzania (or via fax at 0255-27-2751113); (3) KIWAKKUKI, P.O. Box 567, Moshi, Tanza-
    nia; and (4) Tanzania Environmental Action Association, P.O. Box 8098, Moshi, Tanzania
    (or via fax at 0255-27-2751113).

References

Adelman, I. (2001). Fallacies in development theory and their implications for policy. In G. Meier and J. Stiglitz (Eds.), *Frontiers of development economics: The future in perspective* (pp. 103–134). Washington, DC: The World Bank.

Ainsworth, M., Beegle, K., & Nyamete, A. (1995). *The impact of female schooling on fertility and contraceptive use: A study of fourteen Sub-Saharan countries.* Washington, DC: World Bank.

Amin, S. (1982). The disarticulation of the economy within "developing societies." In H. Alavi and T. Shanin (Eds.), *Introduction to the sociology of "developing societies"* (pp. 205–209). London: Macmillan.

Anderson, B. (1983). *Imagined communities.* London and New York: Verso.

Appadurai, A. (1996). *Modernity at large: Cultural dimensions of globalization.* Minneapolis and London: University of Minnesota Press.

Apple, M. W. (1982). *Education and power.* Boston: ARK.

———. (1990). *Ideology and curriculum* (second edition). New York and London: Routledge.

———. (1993). *Official knowledge: Democratic education in a conservative age.* New York and London: Routledge.

Ball, S. J. (1994). *Education reform: A critical and post-structural approach.* Buckingham, UK: Open University Press.

Basu, A. M. (1999). Poverty and AIDS: The vicious circle. In M. Livi-Bacci and G. De Santis (Eds.), *Population and poverty in the developing world* (pp. 144–160). Oxford: Oxford University Press.

Beneria, L., & Sen, G. (1981). Accumulation, reproduction and women's role in economic development: Boserup revisited. *Signs, 7,* 279–298.

Bledsoe, C. (1990). School fees and the marriage process for Mende girls in Sierra Leone. In P. R. Sanday and R. G. Goodenough (Eds.), *Beyond the second sex: New directions in the anthropology of gender* (pp. 284–309). Philadelphia: University of Pennsylvania Press.

Bledsoe, C. H., & Cohen, B. (1993). *Social dynamics of adolescent fertility in Sub-Saharan Africa.* Washington, DC: National Academy Press.

Boli, J., & Ramirez, F. (1992). Compulsory schooling in the western cultural context: Essence and variation. In R. F. Arnove, P. G. Altbach, and G. P. Kelly (Eds.), *Emergent issues in education: Comparative perspectives* (pp. 25–38). Albany: SUNY Press.

Bond, G. C., Kreniske, J., Susser, I., & Vincent, J. (Eds.) (1997). *The anthropology of AIDS in Africa and the Caribbean.* Boulder: Westview.

Boserup, E. (1970). *Woman's role in economic development.* New York: St. Martin's.

Bourdieu, P. (1977). *Outline of a theory of practice.* Cambridge, UK: Cambridge University Press.

Bourdieu, P. (1984). *Distinction: A social critique of the judgement of taste.* Cambridge, MA: Harvard University Press.

Bourdieu, P., & Wacquant, L. (1992). *An invitation to reflexive sociology.* Chicago: The University of Chicago Press.

Bowles, S., & Gintis, H. (1976). *Schooling in capitalist America.* New York: Basic Books.

Boym, S. (2001). *The future of nostalgia.* New York: Basic Books.

Bradley, C. (1995). Women's empowerment and fertility decline in western Kenya. In S. Greenhalgh (Ed.), *Situating fertility: Anthropology and demographic inquiry* (pp. 157–178). Cambridge: Cambridge University Press.

Brock-Utne, B. (2002). *Language, democracy and education in Africa.* Uppsala: Nordiska Afrikainstitutet.

———. (2000). *Whose education for all? The recolonialization of the African mind.* New York and London: Falmer.

"Brown's 'Marshall Plan' for poor countries." (2001, November 27). *BBC News* [Online]. Available at: http://news.bbc.co.uk/1/hi/business/1679585.stm [Retrieved January 12, 2003].

Buchert, L. (1994). *Education in the development of Tanzania, 1919–1990.* London: James Currey.

Bureau of Statistics. (n. date). *1988 Population Census: Preliminary Report.* Dar es Salaam: Ministry of Finance, Economic Affairs and Planning.

Bureau of Statistics. (1990). *Population census: Regional profile, Kilimanjaro.* Dar es Salaam: President's Office, Planning Commission.

———. (1995). *Selected statistics series: 1951–1992.* Dar es Salaam: President's Office, Planning Commission.

Bureau of Statistics Tanzania and Macro International Inc. (1997). *Tanzania demographic and health survey 1996.* Calverton, MD: Bureau of Statistics and Macro International.

Caldwell, J. C. (1998). Mass education and fertility decline. In P. Demeny and G. McNicoll (Eds.), *The reader in population and development* (pp. 42–56). New York: St. Martin's.

Cardoso, F. H., & Faletto, E. (1979). *Dependency and development in Latin America.* Berkeley: University of California Press.

Cleland, J. G., & van Ginneken, J. (1988). Maternal education and child survival in developing countries: The search for pathways of influence. *Social Science and Medicine* 27(12), 1357–1368.

Cochrane, S. H. (1979). *Fertility and education: What do we really know?* Washington, DC: The World Bank.

Colwell, A. S. C. (2001). *Vision and revision: Demography, material and child health development, and the representation of native women in colonial Tanzania.* Unpublished doctoral dissertation, University of Illinois at Urbana-Champaign.

Cooksey, B. (2003). Marketing reform? The rise and fall of agricultural liberalisation in Tanzania. *Development Policy Review* 21(1), 67–91.

Coulson, A. (1982). *Tanzania: A political economy.* New York: Oxford University Press.

Cremin, L. (1978). Family-community linkages in American education: Some comments on the recent historiography. *Teachers College Record* 79(4), 683–704.

Criper, C., & Dodd, W. A. (1984). *Report on the teaching of the English language program and its use as a medium of education in Tanzania, with special reference to the use of British technical cooperation.* Unpublished report.

Currey, J. R. (n. date). *Eleusine cultivation by the Wachagga on Kilimanjaro.* Kilimanjaro (Moshi) District Book, Vol. 1.

Dexter, E. R., LeVine, S. E., & Velasco, P. M. (1998). Maternal schooling and health-related language and literacy skills in rural Mexico. *Comparative Education Review* 42(2), 130–162.

Dundas, C. (1927, May 2). *Letter to The Honorable The Acting Director of Education,* Tanzania National Archives File 10563.

Edwards, M. (1999). *Future positive: International co-operation in the 21ˢᵗ century.* London: Earthscan.

Edwards, M., & Hulme, D. (1998). Too close for comfort? The impact of official aid on nongovernmental organizations. *Current Issues in Comparative Education* 1(1) [Online]. Available at: http://www.tc.columbia.edu/CICE/articles/medh111.htm [Retrieved February 21, 2003].

Elyachar, J. (2002). Empowerment money: The World Bank, non-governmental organizations, and the value of culture in Egypt. *Public Culture* 14(3), 493–513.

Escobar, A. (1995). *Encountering development: The making and unmaking of the Third World.* Princeton: Princeton University Press.

———. (1996). Constructing nature: Elements for a poststructural political economy. In R. Peet and M. Watts (Eds.), *Liberation ecologies: Environment, development, social movements* (pp. 46–68). London and New York: Routledge.

Farmer, P. (1996). Women, poverty, and AIDS. In P. Farmer, M. Connors, and J. Simmons (Eds.), *Women, poverty, and AIDS* (pp. 3–38). Monroe, ME: Common Courage.

———. (1999). *Infections and inequalities: The modern plague.* Berkeley: University of California Press.

Feinberg, W., & Soltis, J. F. (1998). *School and society.* New York and London: Teachers College Press.

Ferguson, J. (1994). *The anti-politics machine: "Development," depoliticization, and bureaucratic power in Lesotho.* Minneapolis and London: University of Minnesota Press.

———. (1999). *Expectations of modernity: Myths and meanings of urban life on the Zambian copperbelt.* Berkeley and Los Angeles: University of California Press.

Fernandez-Kelly, M. P. (1983). *For we are sold, I and my people: Women in industry in Mexico's frontier.* Albany: SUNY Press.

Finnegan, W. (2002, April 8). Letter from Bolivia: Leasing the rain. *The New Yorker,* 43–53.

Fisher, W. F. (1997). Doing good? The politics and antipolitics of NGO practice. *Annual Review of Anthropology,* 26, 439–464.

Foucault, M. (1980). *Power/knowledge: Selected interviews and other writings.* New York: Pantheon.

———. (1991). Politics and the study of discourse. In G. Burchell, C. Gordon, and P. Miller (Eds.), *The Foucault effect: Studies in governmentality* (pp. 53–72). Chicago: The University of Chicago Press.

Fowler, F. J. (1993). *Survey research methods* (second edition). Newbury Park, CA: Sage.

Frank, A. G. (1967). *Sociology of development and underdevelopment of sociology.* London: Pluto.

Fraser, N., & Gordon, L. (1994). A genealogy of dependency: Tracing a keyword of the U.S. welfare state. *Signs* 19(2), 309–336.

Gage, A. J. (2000). Female empowerment and adolescent demographic behaviour. In H. B. Presser and G. Sen (Eds.), *Women's empowerment and demographic processes* (pp. 186–203). Oxford: Oxford University Press.

Gage, A. J., & Bledsoe, C. H. (1994). The effects of education and social stratification on marriage and the transition to parenthood in Freetown, Sierra Leone. In C. H. Bledsoe and G. Pison (Eds.), *Nuptiality in Sub-Saharan Africa: Contemporary anthropological and demographic perspectives* (pp. 148–164). Oxford: Clarendon.

Gandhi, L. (1998). *Postcolonial theory: A critical introduction.* New York: Columbia University Press.

Geilinger, W. (1936). The retreat of the Kilimanjaro glaciers. *Tanganyika Notes and Records,* 2, 7–20.

Gillingham, M. E. (1999). Gaining access to water: Formal and working rules of indigenous irrigation management on Mount Kilimanjaro, Tanzania. *Natural Resources Journal* 39(3), 419–441.

Glewwe, P. (1999). Why does mother's schooling raise child health in developing countries? Evidence from Morocco. *The Journal of Human Resources* 34(1), 124–159.

Gough, D. (2002, February 25). The melting mountain. *Newsweek,* p. 34.

Graff, H. (1979). Literacy, education, and fertility, past and present: A critical review. *Population and Development Review* 5(1), 105–140.

Greene, R. W. (1999). *Malthusian worlds: U.S. leadership and the governing of the population crisis.* Boulder: Westview.

Greenhalgh, S. (1995). Anthropology theorizes reproduction: Integrating practice, political economic, and feminist perspectives. In S. Greenhalgh (Ed.), *Situating fertility: Anthropology and demographic inquiry* (pp. 3–28). Cambridge: Cambridge University Press.

Grove, A. (1993). Water use by the Chagga on Kilimanjaro. *African Affairs* 92(368), 431–448.

Gupta, A. (1998). *Postcolonial developments: Agriculture in the making of modern India.* Durham, NC, and London: Duke University Press.

Gutmann, B. (1926). *Das recht der Dschagga* [Translated by A. M. Nagler]. Human Relations Area Files.

————. (1932 [1958]). *The tribal teachings of the Chagga, volume 1* [Translated by W. Goodenough and D. Crawford]. Human Relations Area Files.

Hall, S., Critcher, C., Jefferson, T., Clarke, J., & Roberts, B. (1978). *Policing the crisis: Mugging, the state, and law and order.* New York: Holmes and Meier.

Hartsock, N. (1990). Foucault on power: A theory for women? In L. J. Nicholson (Ed.), *Feminism/postmodernism* (pp. 157–175). New York and London: Routledge.

Heilman, B. (1998). Who are the indigenous Tanzanians? Competing conceptions of Tanzanian citizenship in the business community. *Africa Today* 45(3–4), 369–387.

Higgens, M. (2001, February 22). Global warming thaws tropical ice caps. *Environmental News Network* [Online]. Available at: http://www.enn.com/news/enn-stories/2001/02/02222001/kilimanjaro_42131.asp [Retrieved February 7, 2003].

Hollos, M. (1991). Migration, education, and the status of women in southern Nigeria. *American Anthropologist* 93(4), 852–870.

Hollos, M., & Larsen, U. (1997). From lineage to conjugality: The social context of fertility decisions among the Pare of northern Tanzania. *Social Science and Medicine* 45(3), 361–372.

Howard, M. T., & Millard, A. V. (1997). *Hunger and shame: Poverty and child malnutrition on Mount Kilimanjaro.* New York and London: Routledge.

Huntington, S. P. (1968). *Political order in changing societies.* New Haven: Yale University Press.

Hyden, G. (1980). *Beyond ujamaa in Tanzania: Underdevelopment and an uncaptured peasantry.* Berkeley: University of California Press.

Inkeles, A. (1998). *One world emerging? Convergence and divergence in industrial societies.* Boulder: Westview.

Inkeles, A., & Smith, D. H. (1974). *Becoming modern: Individual change in six developing countries.* Cambridge, MA: Harvard University Press.

Intergovernmental Panel on Climate Change. (1998). *The regional impacts of climate change.* Cambridge and New York: Cambridge University Press.

"Invitation from the King of Chagga." (1878, July). *Church Missionary Intelligencer and Record,* p. 448.

Jacobs, M. (1994). The limits to neoclassicism: Towards an institutional environmental economics. In M. Redclift and T. Benton (Eds.), *Social theory and the global environment* (pp. 67–91). London and New York: Routledge.

Jejeebhoy, S. J. (1995). *Women's education, autonomy, and reproductive behaviour: Experience from developing countries.* Oxford: Clarendon.

Jennings, M. (2001). 'Development is a very political thing in Tanzania': Oxfam & the Chunya Integrated Development Programme: 1972–76. In O. Barrow and M. Jennings (Eds.), *The charitable impulse: NGOs and development in East and North-East Africa* (pp. 109–132). Oxford: James Currey and Bloomfield, CT: Kumarian.

Johnston, P. H. (1946). *Some notes on land tenure on Kilimanjaro and the vihamba of the Wachagga.* Kilimanjaro (Moshi) District Book, Vol. 1.

Jones, P. W. (1997). On World Bank education financing. *Comparative Education* 33(1), 117–129.

Kabeer, N. (1994). *Reversed realities: Gender hierarchies in development thought.* New York: Verso.

Kamat, S. (2002). *Development hegemony: NGOs and the state in India.* New Delhi: Oxford University Press.

Kapiga, S., Hunter, D., & Nachtigal, G. (1992). Reproductive knowledge, and contraceptive awareness and practice among secondary school pupils in Bagamoyo and Dar-es-Salaam, Tanzania. *Central African Journal of Medicine 38*(9), 375–380.

Kelsall, T. (2001). Donors, NGOs & the state: Governance & 'civil society' in Tanzania. In O. Barrow and M. Jennings (Eds.), *The charitable impulse: NGOs and development in East and North-East Africa* (pp. 133–148). Oxford: James Currey and Bloomfield, CT: Kumarian.

Kelsall, T., & Mercer, C. (2002). *Empowering the people? World Vision and 'transformatory development' in Tanzania.* Unpublished manuscript.

Kitururu, M. (1996, July 25). Secondary school fees hiked. *Daily News* (Tanzania), p. 1.

Knodel, J. (2003). The closing of the gender gap in schooling: The case of Thailand. In E. R. Beauchamp (Ed.), *Comparative education reader* (pp. 183–215). New York and London: RoutledgeFalmer.

Komba-Malekela, B., & Liljestrom, R. (1994). Looking for men. In Z. Tumbo-Masabo and R. Liljestrom (Eds.), *Chelewa, chelewa: The dilemma of teenage girls* (pp. 133–149). Sweden: The Scandinavian Institute of African Studies.

Kristof, N. (2002, July 5). Farm subsidies that kill. *The New York Times*, p. A19.

Kumar, A. (1992). *On their own two feet: Women and reproduction in Rajasthan.* Unpublished doctoral dissertation, University of North Carolina-Chapel Hill.

Larsen, U. (1996). Childlessness, subfertility, and infertility in Tanzania. *Studies in Family Planning* 27(1), 18–28.

Lassibille, G., Tan, J-P, & Sumra, S. (2000). Expansion of private secondary education: Lessons from recent experience in Tanzania. *Comparative Education Review* 44(1), 1–28.

Lema, A. A. (1968). The Lutheran church's contribution to education in Kilimanjaro 1893–1933. *Tanganyika Notes and Records*, 68, 87–94.

LeVine, R. A. (1999). Literacy and population change. In D. A. Wagner, Venezky, R. L, and Street, B. V. (Eds.), *Literacy: An international handbook* (pp. 300–305). Boulder: Westview.

LeVine, R. A., LeVine, S. E., Richman, A., Uribe, F. M. T., Correa, C. S., & Miller, P. M. (1991). Women's schooling and child care in the demographic transition: A Mexican case study. *Population and Development Review* 17(3), 459–496.

Levinson, B., & Holland, D. (1996). The cultural production of the educated person: An introduction. In B. A. Levinson, D. E. Foley, and D. C. Holland (Eds.), *The cultural production of the educated person: Critical ethnographies of schooling and local practice* (pp. 1–54). Albany: SUNY Press.

Levinson, B. A. U., & Sutton, M. (2001). Introduction: Policy as/in practice—A sociocultural approach to the study of educational policy. In M. Sutton and B. Levinson (Eds.), *Policy as practice: Toward a comparative sociocultural analysis of educational policy* (pp. 1–22). Westport, CT: Ablex.

Lloyd, C. B., & Blanc, A. K. (1996). Children's schooling in sub-Saharan Africa: The role of father, mothers, and others. *Population and Development Review* 22(2), 265–298.

Lutz, C., & Collins, J. (1993). *Reading National Geographic.* Chicago: University of Chicago Press.

Maarifa ni Ufunguo [Knowledge Is the Key]. (2001). *Cost sharing: A case study of education in Kilimanjaro.* Unpublished manuscript. Arusha, Tanzania.

Maganga, F. P., Butterworth, J. A., & Moriarty, P. (2002). Domestic water supply, competition for water resources and IRWM in Tanzania: A review and discussion paper. *Physics and Chemistry of the Earth,* 27, 919–926.

Mahmud, S., & Johnston, A. M. (1994). Women's status, empowerment, and reproductive outcomes. In G. Sen, A. Germain, and L. C. Chen (Eds.), *Population policies reconsidered: Health, empowerment, and rights* (pp. 151–159). Boston: Harvard School of Public Health.

Malekela, G. A. (1983). *Access to secondary education in Sub-Saharan Africa: The Tanzanian experiment.* Unpublished doctoral dissertation, University of Chicago.

Markee, N. (1997). *Managing curricular innovations.* New York: Cambridge University Press.

Maro, P. S. (1974). *Population and land resources in Northern Tanzania: The dynamics of change 1920–1970.* Unpublished doctoral dissertation, University of Minnesota.

Mason, K. O. (1984). *The status of women: A review of its relationships to fertility and morality.* New York: Rockefeller.

Matasha, E., Ntembelea, T., Mayaud, P., Saida, W., Todd, J., Mujaya, B., & Tendo-Wambua, L. (1998). Sexual and reproductive health among primary and secondary school pupils in Mwanza, Tanzania: Need for intervention. *AIDS CARE* 10(5), 571–582.

Mbilinyi, M. (1998). Searching for utopia: The politics of gender and education in Tanzania. In M. N. Bloch, J. A. Beoku-Betts, and B. R. Tabachnick (Eds.), *Women and education in Sub-Saharan Africa: Power, opportunities, and constraints* (pp. 277–295). Boulder: Lynne Rienner.

McClelland, DC (1961). *The achieving society.* Princeton: Van Nostrand.

McMichael, P. (1996). *Development and social change: A global perspective.* Thousand Oaks, CA: Pine Forge.

Meier, G. M. (2001). The old generation of development economists and the new. In G. M. Meier and J. E. Stiglitz (Eds.), *Frontiers of development economics* (pp. 13–50). Washington, DC: The World Bank.

Meyer, H. (1891). *Across East African glaciers: An account of the first ascent of Kilimanjaro.* London: George Philip & Son.

Meyer, J. W., Ramirez, F. O., Rubinson, R., & Boli-Bennett, J. (1977). The world education revolution 1950–1970. *Sociology of Education,* 50, 242–258.

Ministry of Education. (1982). *Some basic facts about education in Tanzania.* Dar es Salaam: Ministry of Education.

Ministry of Education and Culture. (1995a). *Education and training policy.* Dar es Salaam: Ministry of Education and Culture.

———. (1995b). *Girls secondary education support: Design.* Dar es Salaam: Ministry of Education and Culture.

———. (1996). *Basic education statistics in Tanzania (BEST): 1994 regional data.* Dar es Salaam: Ministry of Education and Culture.

———. (1999). *Basic education statistics in Tanzania (BEST): 1994–1998 national data.* Dar es Salaam: Ministry of Education and Culture.

———. (2001). *Family life education for secondary schools: Teacher's guide—Civics.* Dar es Salaam: Ministry of Education and Culture.

Mnyika, K. S., Kvale, G., & Klepp, K.-I. (1995a). Perceived function of and barriers to condom use in Arusha and Kilimanjaro regions of Tanzania. *AIDS Care* 7(3), 295–305.

Mnyika, K. S., Klepp, K. I., Kvale, G., Schreiner, A., & Seha, A. M. (1995b). Condom awareness and use in the Arusha and Kilimanjaro regions, Tanzania: A population-based study. *AIDS Education and Prevention* 7(5), 403–414.

Mohanty, C. T. (1991). Under western eyes: Feminist scholarship and colonial discourses. In C. T. Mohanty, A. Russo, and L. Torres (Eds.), *Third world women and the politics of feminism* (pp. 51–80). Bloomington: Indiana University Press.

Moore, S. F. (1986). *Social facts and fabrications: "Customary" law on Kilimanjaro, 1880–1980.* Cambridge, UK and New York: Cambridge University Press.

———. (1996). Introduction. In *Chagga childhood: A description of indigenous education in an East African tribe* [reprint] (pp. ix–xx). Munster-Hamburg: LIT.

Moser, C. (1989). Gender planning in the Third World: Meeting practical and strategic gender needs. *World Development* 17(11), 1799–1825.

Mosgrove, D. L. (1998). *Watering African moons: Culture and history of irrigation design on Kilimanjaro and beyond.* Unpublished doctoral dissertation, Cornell University.

Moshi, C. A. (1994). *A comprehensive report on a local government elections study done in Old Moshi East Ward- Moshi Rural District in September/October, 1994.* Dar es Salaam: Unpublished report.

Mtesigwa, P. (2001). *Tanzania's educational language policy: The medium of instruction at the secondary level.* Unpublished doctoral dissertation, Teachers College, Columbia University.

Mumford, W. B. (1929). Education and the social adjustment of the primitive peoples of Africa to European culture. *Africa* II(2), 138–159.

———. (1930). Malangali School. *Africa* III(3), 265–290.

Mutua, K., & Swadener, B. B. (forthcoming). *Decolonizing research in cross-cultural contexts: Critical personal narratives.* New York: SUNY Press.

Nash, J. M. (2001, August 20). America's best: The iceman. *Time,* pp. 42–43.

National Bureau of Statistics. (2002). Household budget survey 2000/01 [Online]. Available at: http://www.tanzania.go.tz/statisticsf.html [Retrieved September 24, 2002].

National Bureau of Statistics and Macro International. (2000). *Tanzania reproductive and child health survey 1999.* Dar es Salaam: National Bureau of Statistics; Calverton, MD: Macro International Inc.

Native agriculture: Moshi District. (n. date; around 1945). Kilimanjaro (Moshi) District Book, Volume I.

New, C. (1873 [1970]). *Life, wanderings, and labours in eastern Africa.* London: Frank Cass and Company Limited.

Ngatara, L. A. (2001, March 17). Doomsday for Kilimanjaro people in sight. *The Guardian* (Tanzania), n. page.

Nyerere, J. K. (1962 [1968]). Ujamaa: The basis of African socialism. In J. K. Nyerere (Ed.), *Ujamaa: Essays on socialism* (pp. 1–12). Dar es Salaam: Oxford University Press.

———. (1967a [1968]). The Arusha Declaration. In J. K. Nyerere (Ed.), *Ujamaa: Essays on socialism* (pp. 13–37). Dar es Salaam: Oxford University Press.

———. (1967b [1968]). Education for self-reliance. *Ujamaa: Essays on socialism* (pp. 44–75). Dar es Salaam: Oxford University Press.

Ong, A. (1987). *Spirits of resistance and capitalist discipline: Factory women in Malaysia.* Albany: SUNY Press.

Onishi, N. (2000, April 14). AIDS cuts swath through Africa's teachers. *The New York Times,* pp. A1, A6.

Parpart, J. L., & Marchand, M. H. (1995). Exploding the canon. In M. H. Marchand and J. L. Parpart (Eds.), *Feminism/postmodernism/development* (pp. 1–22). New York: Routledge.

Peet, R. (with E. Hartwick). (1999). *Theories of development.* New York and London: Guilford.

Pennycook, A. (1998). *English and the discourses of colonialism.* London and New York: Routledge.

Peterson, R. B. (2000). *Conversations in the rainforest: Culture, values, and the environment in Central Africa.* Boulder: Westview.

Pigg, S. L. (1992). Inventing social categories through place: Social representations and development in Nepal. *Society for Comparative Study of Society and History* 34(3), 491–513.

———. (1997). Found in most traditional societies: Traditional medical practitioners between culture and development. In F. Cooper and R. Packard (Eds.), *International development and the social sciences: Essays on the history and politics of knowledge* (pp. 259–290). Berkeley: University of California Press.

Pitman, G. K. (2002). *Bridging troubled waters: Assessing the World Bank water resource strategy.* Washington, DC: The World Bank.

Ponte, S. (1998). Fast crops, fast cash: Market liberalization and rural livelihoods in Songea and Morogoro Districts, Tanzania. *Canadian Journal of African Studies* 32(2), 316–348.

Popkewitz, T. S. (1984). *Paradigm & ideology in educational research.* London and New York: Falmer.

———. (Ed.) (1993). *Changing patterns of power: Social regulation and teacher education reform.* Albany: SUNY Press.

———. (2000). Globalization/regionalization, knowledge, and the educational practices. In T. S. Popkewitz (Ed.), *Educational knowledge: Changing relationships between the state, civil society, and the educational community* (pp. 3–27). Albany: SUNY Press.

Qoheleth Foundation. (2002, February). *Progress and financial report for the period up to December 2001.* Moshi: The Qoheleth Foundation.

Ramirez, F. O., & Boli, J. (1987). The political construction of mass education: European origins and worldwide institutionalization. *Sociology of Education,* 60, 2–17.

Raphael, L. (2001). Language teaching in tatters—BAKITA. *Sunday Observer* [Online]. Available at: http://www.ippmedia.com/observer/2001/07/08/observer7.asp [Retrieved July 8, 2001].

Rees, W. E. (2001). *Economics and sustainability: Conflict or convergence? (An ecological economics perspective)* [Online]. Paper presented at the StatsCan Economic Conference, Ottawa, June 5, 2001. Available at: http: www.environomics.org/environomics/econSustain.pdf [Retrieved January 26, 2003].

Report by His Britannic Majesty's government to the Council of the League of Nations on the administration of Tanganyika Territory for the year 1925. (1926). London: Colonial Office.

Richey, L. A. (1999). *"Development," gender and family planning: Population politics and the Tanzanian national population policy.* Unpublished doctoral dissertation, University of North Carolina-Chapel Hill.

———. (2001). Does economic policy conflict with population policy? A case study of reproductive health in Tanzania. Working paper 01.7. Copenhagen: Centre for Development Research.

———. (2002). *From the politics to the clinics: Population and women's reproductive health in Tanzania.* Paper presented at the IUSSP Committee on Anthropological Demography Seminar on Macro-Meso-Micro Social Influences in Health: Changing Patterns of Morbidity and Mortality, Yaounde, Cameroon, June 5–8.

Rogers, B. (1980). *The domestication of women: Discrimination in developing societies.* New York: St. Martin's.

Rogers, S. G. (1972). *The search for political focus on Kilimanjaro: A history of Chagga politics, 1916–1952, with special reference to the cooperative movement and indirect rule.* Unpublished doctoral dissertation, University of Dar es Salaam.

Rostow, W. W. (1960). *The stages of economic growth: A non-communist manifesto.* Cambridge, UK: Cambridge University Press.

Rothenberg, D. A. (2001). *Positioned perspectives: Understanding childhood malnutrition in Niger.* Unpublished doctoral dissertation, Michigan State University.

Rugumisa, S. (1989). *A review of the Tanzanian economic recovery programme.* Dar es Salaam: TADREG.

Said, E. W. (1978). *Orientalism.* New York: Vintage Books.

Samoff, J. (1987). School expansion in Tanzania: Private initiatives and public policy. *Comparative Education Review* 31(3), 333–360.

———. (1990). "Modernizing" a socialist vision: Education in Tanzania. In M. Carnoy and J. Samoff (Eds.), *Education and social transition in the Third World* (pp. 209–273). Princeton: Princeton University Press.

———. (Ed.) (1994). *Coping with crisis: Austerity, adjustment and human resources.* Paris: UNESCO.

———. (1999). *No teacher guide, no textbooks, no chairs: Contending with crisis in African education.* Paper presented at the 43rd Annual Meeting of the African Studies Association, November 11–14.

Schoepf, B. G. (1998). Inscribing the body politic: Women and AIDS in Africa. In M. Lock and P. A. Kaufert (Eds.), *Pragmatic women and body politics* (pp. 98–126). Cambridge, UK: Cambridge University Press.

Schriewer, J. (2000). World system and interrelationship networks: The internationalization of education and the role of comparative inquiry. In T. S. Popkewitz (Ed.), *Educational knowledge: Changing relations between the state, civil society, and the educational community* (pp. 305–343). New York: SUNY Press.

Schultz, T. W. (1998). Population effects of the value of human time. In P. Demeny and G. McNicoll (Eds.), *The reader in population and development* (pp. 37–41). New York: St. Martin's.

Sen, A. K. (1999). *Development as freedom.* New York: Knopf.

Sen, G., Germain, A., & Chen, L. C. (1994). *Population policies reconsidered: Health, empowerment, and rights.* Boston: Harvard University Press.

Serpell, R. (1993). *The significance of schooling: Life-journeys in an African society.* Cambridge, UK and New York: Cambridge University Press.

Setel, P. (1995). *Bo'n town life: Youth, AIDS, and the changing character of adulthood in Kilimanjaro, Tanzania.* Unpublished doctoral dissertation, Boston University.

———. (1999). *A plague of paradoxes: AIDS, culture, and demography in northern Tanzania.* Chicago: University of Chicago Press.

Shann, G. N. (1956). The early development of education among the Chagga. *Tanganyika Notes and Records, 45,* 21–32.

Shao, I. (Ed.) (1992). *Structural adjustment in a socialist country: The case of Tanzania.* Harare: Sapes.

Shapiro, I., & Birdsall, N. (2002, March 20). *How does the proposed level of foreign economic aid under the Bush budget compare with historical levels? And what would be the effects of Bush's New 'Millennium Challenge Account'?* Center for Global Development and Center on Budget and Policy Priorities [Online]. Available at: http://www.cbpp.org/3-14-02foreignaid.htm [Retrieved January 12, 2003].

Sharma, N. P., Damhaug, T., Gilgan-Hunt, E., Grey, D., Okaru, V., & Rothberg, D. (1996). *African water resources: Challenges and opportunities for sustainable development.* Washington, DC: The World Bank.

Sharp, L. A. (2002). *The sacrificed generation: Youth, history, and the colonized mind in Madagascar.* Berkeley: University of California Press.

Shore, C., & Wright, S. (Eds.) (1997). *Anthropology of policy: Critical perspectives on governance and power.* London and New York: Routledge.

Simmons, J., Farmer, P., & Schoepf, B. G. (1996). A global perspective. In P. Farmer, M. Connors, and J. Simmons (Eds.), *Women, poverty and AIDS: Sex, drugs and structural violence* (pp. 39–90). Monroe, ME: Common Courage.

Smith, A. (1970). Introduction to the third edition. In C. New's *Life, wanderings, and labours in Eastern Africa.* London: Frank Cass and Company Limited.

So, A. Y. (1990). *Social change and development: Modernization, dependency, and world-system theories.* Newbury Park, CA: Sage.

Spivak, G. C. (1999). *A critique of post-colonial reason: Toward a history of the vanishing present.* Cambridge, MA and London: Harvard University Press.

Stahl, K. (1964). *History of the Chagga people of Kilimanjaro.* London and Paris: Mouton & Co.

Stambach, A. (1994). "Here in Africa, we teach; students listen": Lessons about culture from Tanzania. *Journal of Curriculum and Supervision* 9(4), 368–385.

———. (2000). *Lessons from Mount Kilimanjaro: Schooling, community, and gender in East Africa.* New York: Routledge.

Steeves, H. L. (1997). *Gender violence and the press: The St. Kizito story.* Athens, OH: Ohio University Press.

Stiglitz, J. (2002). *Globalization and its discontents.* New York: Norton.

Stromquist, N. P. (Ed.) (1992). *Women and education in Latin America: Knowledge, power, and change.* Boulder: Lynne Rienner.

———. (1998). Agents in women's education: Some trends in the African context.. In M. N. Bloch, J. A. Beoku-Betts, and B. R. Tabachnick (Eds.), *Women and education in Sub-Saharan Africa:: Power, opportunities, and constraints* (pp. 25–46). Boulder: Lynne Rienner.

———. (1999). The impact of structural adjustment programs in Africa and Asia. In C. Heward and S. Bunwaree (Eds.), *Gender, education, and development: Beyond access to empowerment* (pp. 17–32). London and New York: Zed.

Superintendent of Education. (1928, July 4). *Correspondence with the Chief Secretary about the school at Old Moshi.* Secretariat File # 12424, Vol. I, Tanzania National Archives.

Sutton, M. (2001). Policy research as ethnographic refusal: The case of women's literacy in Nepal. In M. Sutton and B. Levinson (Eds.), *Policy as practice: Toward a comparative sociocultural analysis of educational policy* (pp. 77–99). Westport, CT: Ablex.

Swainson, N., Bendera, S., Gordon, R., & Kadzamira, E. (1998). *Promoting girls' education in Africa: The design and implementation of policy interventions.* London: Department for International Development.

TADREG. (1990, July). *Girls' educational opportunities & performance in Tanzania.* Dar es Salaam: TADREG.

Tanzania Gender Networking Programme (TGNP). (1993). *Gender profile of Tanzania.* Dar es Salaam: TGNP.

Taylor, S., Rizvi, F., Lingard, B., & Henry, M. (Eds.) (1997). *Educational policy and the politics of change.* London and New York: Routledge.

Therkildsen, O. (1988). *Watering white elephants? Lessons from donor funded planning and implementation of rural water supplies in Tanzania.* Uppsala: Scandinavian Institute of African Studies.

Thomas, N. (1994). *Colonialism's culture: Anthropology, travel, and government.* Princeton: Princeton University Press.

Todaro, M. P. (1989). *Economic development in the Third World.* New York and London: Longman.

Tripp, A. M. (1997). *Changing the rules: The politics of liberalization and the urban informal economy in Tanzania.* Berkeley: University of California Press.

Turshen, M. (1999). *Privatizing health services in Africa.* New Brunswick, NJ and London: Rutgers University Press.

Tyack, D., & Cuban, L. (1995). *Tinkering toward utopia: A century of public school reform.* Cambridge, MA and London: Harvard University Press.

UNAIDS. (2002). *United Republic of Tanzania epidemiological fact sheet on HIV/AIDS and sexually transmitted infections, 2002 update* [Online]. Available at: http://www.unaids.org/hivaidsinfo/statistics/fact_sheets/pdfs/Tanzania_en.pdf [Retrieved December 12, 2002].

UNESCO. (2000). *The Dakar framework for action.* Paris: UNESCO.

UNICEF. (1999). *The state of the world's children 1999.* New York: UNICEF.

———. (2000a). *The progress of nations 2000.* New York: UNICEF.

———. (2000b). *Tanzania 2000 annual report.* New York: Unpublished report.

Union of Moshi Rural Non-Governmental Organisations (UMRU-NGO). (2001, January). *Constitution and Rules.* Unpublished report.

United Nations. (1994). *Agenda 21: Programme of action for sustainable development.* New York: United Nations Publications.

———. (1995). *Population and development: Programme of action adopted at the International Conference on Population and Development, Cairo, 5–13 September 1994.* New York: United Nations Publications.

United Republic of Tanzania. (2000). *Poverty reduction and rural water supply.* Dar es Salaam: Ministry of Water.

———. (2001a, March). *The contributions of the water and livestock sectors in eradicating poverty in the country.* Speech by the Minister of Water and Livestock Development. Dar es Salaam: Ministry of Water and Livestock Development.

———. (2001b). *The national policy on non-governmental organizations (NGOs).* Dar es Salaam: Vice President's Office.

———. (2002). 2002 Population and housing census [Online]. Available at: http://www.tanzania.go.tz/2002census.html. [Retrieved January 20, 2003].

Unterhalter, E. (2000). Transnational visions of the 1990s. In M. Arnot and J. Dillabough (Eds.), *Challenging democracy: International perspectives on gender, education and citizenship* (pp. 87–102). London and New York: Routledge.

Vandemoortele, J. (2000). *Absorbing social shocks, protecting children and reducing poverty: The role of basic human services* (Staff Working Papers EPP-00-001). New York: UNICEF.

Van de Walle, N. (2001). *African economies and the politics of permanent crisis, 1979–1999.* Cambridge, UK and New York: Cambridge University Press.

Vavrus, F. (1998). *Schooling, fertility, and the discourse of development: A study of the Kilimanjaro region of Tanzania.* Unpublished doctoral dissertation, University of Wisconsin-Madison.

———. (2002a). Making distinctions: Privatization and the (un)educated girl on Mount Kilimanjaro, Tanzania. *International Journal of Educational Development, 22,* 527–547.

———. (2002b). Postcoloniality and English: Exploring language policy and the politics of development in Tanzania. *TESOL Quarterly 36(3),* 373–397.

———. (2002c). Uncoupling the articulation between girls' education and tradition in Tanzania. *Gender and Education 14(4),* 367–389.

———. (forthcoming). The referential web: Externalization beyond education in Tanzania. In G. Steiner-Khamsi (Ed.), *Lessons from elsewhere: The politics of educational borrowing and lending.* New York: Teachers College Press.

Vines, D. (2001). Comment. In G. M. Meier and J. E. Stiglitz (Eds.), *Frontiers of development economics* (pp. 135–146). Washington, DC: The World Bank.

Wagao, J. H. (1990). *Adjustment policies in Tanzania, 1981–1989: The impact of growth, structure and human welfare.* Florence, Italy: Unicef International Child Development Centre.

Whyte, S. R. (1997). *Questioning misfortune: The pragmatics of uncertainty in eastern Uganda.* Cambridge: Cambridge University Press.

The World Bank. (1994). *Tanzania: Agriculture.* Washington, DC: The World Bank.

———. (1996). *Staff appraisal report: River basin management and smallholder irrigation improvement project* (report number 15122-TA). Africa Region: East Africa Department.

———. (1999). *Tanzania: Social sector review.* Washington, DC: The World Bank.

———. (2000). *Agriculture in Tanzania since 1986: Follower or leader of growth?* Washington, DC: The World Bank.

———. (2001). *World development report 2000/2001.* New York: Oxford University Press.

———. (2002). *Education and HIV/AIDS: A window of hope.* Washington, DC: The World Bank.

Wright, M. (1968). Local roots of policy in German East Africa. *Journal of African History* IX(4), 621–630).

Young, R. (1990). *White mythologies: Writing history and the West.* London and New York: Routledge.

Index

Aid
    international, 137, 148–149, 151 n. 1
AIDS, 89–108 passim
    education programs, 36, 37–38, 91–
        92, 107, 139, 141, 142–145
    in Tanzania, 89–90, 92–94, 104–105
    orphans, 139, 143–145
Appadurai, Arjun, 8, 19, 85, 134
Apple, Michael, 44 n. 6
Arusha Declaration, 54, 58

Bledsoe, Carolyn, 96
    and Barney Cohen, 5
    and Anastasia Gage, 96
Bonde Village, 13–14, 16, 18, 109, 118–
        120, 128
Boym, Svetlana, 8–9, 134

Capitalism, 27
    global, 6, 28, 30, 133
Chagga, 46–53, 56, 63, 110–112
    cultural identity, 67–68, 71, 85–86,
        124
    Native Authority, 52, 53, 112
    parents' views, 8–9, 53, 56–57, 72, 83–
        86, 121–123
Chama Cha Mapinduzi (CCM), 54
Coffee, 52, 56, 60, 64 n. 5, 121
    farming, 48–49, 94
    see also Chagga, Kilimanjaro Native
        Cooperative Union
Colonialism
    see Old Moshi
Colwell, Stacie, 36, 51, 52, 64 n. 2, 66
Cremin, Lawrence, 23 n. 5
Crisis
    concept of, 34, 126
    economic, 35, 56, 59–60
Cuban, Larry, 7

Culture, 35–37, 40–41, 66–72
    as cause, 36–37, 51
    as cure, 36–37, 51
    see also Chagga
Currey, J. R., 111
Curriculum, 44 n. 6
    at mission schools, 48
    environmental, 146
    reproductive health and family life,
        36–37, 72–74, 75–77

Debt
    see Development
Decentralization, 33, 42, 115
Dependency theory, 28
Development
    debt and, 32, 148–149
    human, 6
    international, 6, 32, 56, 137, 148–149
    see also Developmentalism
Developmentalism, 6–7, 31–35, 42, 114,
        133, 150
    see also Development
Dundas, Charles, 51, 52, 66

Education
    as panacea, 7, 9, 40–41, 45, 83, 87,
        107, 130
    definition of, 23 n. 5
    'educated persons', 9, 85, 95, 105, 107,
        134
    global models of, 4
    see also AIDS, Schooling
Education for Self-Reliance, 55, 58
Education policies, 43 n. 2, 51–52, 56, 58,
        61, 63
    Education and Training Policy, 60, 63
    pregnancy and, 70–72, 81
    see also Swahili

Edwards, Michael, 148
Employment, 60, 93–94, 99, 100–102, 106–
    107
Empowerment
    of communities, 33, 41–42, 125–126
    of women, 34, 39, 41–42, 44 n. 7, 66,
        73, 83, 85, 142
Environment
    conservation of, 139, 145–146
    degradation of, 84–85, 122–123, 125
    see also Curriculum
Escobar, Arturo, 6–7
Evangelical Lutheran Church of Tanzania
    (ELCT), 1, 10, 69

Family planning, 71–72, 78–80, 103–105
    abortion, 78–82
    see also Curriculum
Farmer, Paul, 90, 107
Feminist modern, 40–41, 105
Ferguson, James, 97, 134, 136, 147, 149–
    150
Foya, Jacob, 111, 128, 131 n. 1, 146–147
Fraser, Nancy, 30
Functionalism, 26–27, 28, 29, 36
Furrows, 46–47, 110–112, 131 n. 7
    furrow societies, 9, 110, 113, 123,
        127–128
    see also Water

Gandhi, Leela, 5–6, 24 n. 6
Gender
    equality in schools, 5, 58–59
    relations, 5, 30, 33–34, 58, 100–101,
        142
Gender and Development (GAD), 29–30,
    34
Gordon, Linda, 30
Greene, Ronald, 40–41, 105
Gupta, Akhil, 6, 123, 130, 131 n. 4, 134
Gutmann, Bruno, 49–50, 66, 67

Hall, Stuart, 34
Hollos, Marida, 83
Human capital theory, 6, 27, 32, 37–39

Imagination, 7–10, 19, 85, 134

International Conference on Population
    and   Development (ICPD), 35–
    40, 43 n. 4, 44 n. 7
International Monetary Fund (IMF), 32, 59,
    63
Irrigation
    see Furrows

Jacobs, Michael, 116, 130
Johnston, P. H., 111, 112
Jomtien,
    see World Conference on Education
    for All
Jones, Philip, 33

Kihamba, 1, 12, 49, 53, 110, 111, 112, 121,
    122
    see also Chagga
Kilimanjaro Native Cooperative Union
    (KNCU), 52
Kilimanjaro Region, 48, 53, 56, 98, 112
    AIDS in, 92–93, 106, 142
    enrollment data, 10, 53, 57–58, 84, 94
    fertility rates, 10, 12
    health services, 10
    NGOs in, 138
    see also Education, Schooling
Kilimanjaro Women's Group Against
    AIDS (KIWAKKUKI), 142–
    145, 151 n. 2

Larsen, Ulla, 12, 83
Liberalization
    of agriculture sector, 60, 114

Maisha magumu, 2, 6, 9, 60, 82–87, 101, 122
Marealle, Chief, 47
Mbali Village, 13–14, 16, 118–123, 127
Meier, Gerald, 32
Merinyo, Joseph, 52
Methods of research, 14–20, 78, 137–138,
    147–148, 149–150
Meyer, Hans, 46–47, 110–111

Missionaries
    American, 50–51
    British, 47
    German, 46–47, 49–51
Miti Village, 13–14, 16, 118–120, 122, 127,
    128
Mkombozi Vocational Training Centre,
    140–142, 151 n. 2
Modernization, 51–52
    theories of, 26–27, 29, 31
Mohanty, Chandra, 29, 30, 41, 137
Moore, Sally Falk, 46, 66, 111, 131 n. 5
Mosgrove, Donald, 131 n. 6

Neoliberalism, 31–35, 41, 63, 116, 130
Neo-Marxism, 28–29, 30, 43 n. 3
New, Charles, 46
Njema Secondary School, 1, 13, 61, 75, 95,
    97–98
Non-governmental organizations (NGOs),
    16, 63, 91, 115, 136–146, 147–
    148
Northern Province, 53
    see Kilimanjaro Region
Nostalgia, 8–10, 18–19, 123
Nyerere, Julius, 54–55, 58, 113

Old Moshi, 10–20, 23 n. 1, 68–69, 109,
    110, 131 n. 5, 142–145
    British era, 49–53
    geography of, 1, 12–13, 117–118
    German era, 47–49, 68
    pre-colonial history, 46–47
    population of, 12–13
    schooling in, 12, 52, 118–121
    see also Furrows, Water

Pennycook, Alastair, 24 n. 6
Peterson, Richard, 14, 15
Popkewitz, Thomas, 24 n. 8, 43 n. 1, 44 n.
    8
Population, 12, 34, 64 n. 2, 122
    desired number of children, 2, 82–84
    land pressure and, 2
    women's education and, 4–5, 9, 51,
    65–66

Postcolonial condition, 5–7, 24 n. 6, 30, 67
Postmodernism, 29–31
Privatization, 32, 60
    in agriculture sector, 114
    in education sector, 60–61, 96–97
    in water sector, 114–116, 129

Qoheleth Foundation, 138–140, 151 n. 2

Rebmann, J. L., 46
Rindi, Chief, 46–47, 118
    descendents of, 47, 52, 111
Richey, Lisa, 12, 82, 88 n. 2
Rogers, Susan (Geiger), 47, 48–49, 51

Sadik, Nafis, 40
Said, Edward, 35, 39, 43–44 n. 5
Samoff, Joel, 31, 63
Schooling
    desire for, 3–4, 7–10, 121, 134
    enrollment data, 4, 55, 57–58, 59, 62,
      90, 96–97, 131 n. 3
    fees for, 1–2, 61, 96, 97–99, 121
    for girls and women, 31, 32–34, 37–
      39, 53
    postsecondary, 3, 100–101
    primary, 3, 55, 88 n. 4, 106
    secondary, 3, 61, 62, 96–97
    sponsorship for, 96–100
    Tanzanian system of, 3, 74
    see also Education, Gender
Schultz, Theodore, 27
Serpell, Robert, 106
Setel, Philip, 13, 93–94, 103, 108 n. 1, n. 4,
    142
Sokoni Village, 13–14, 16, 119–120
Stahl, Kathleen, 1, 47, 111, 131 n. 1
Stambach, Amy, 7, 24 n. 9, 74, 77–78, 88 n.
    1, n. 6, 95, 97
Stiglitz, Joseph, 32, 148–149
Stromquist, Nelly, 28, 108 n. 2
Structural Adjustment Programs (SAPs),
    32, 37, 59–60, 91, 96–97, 99, 107,
    108 n. 2, 114
Swahili
    language, 88 n. 5

language policy, 74, 77–78
    see also Education policy

Tanzania African National Union (TANU),
        54, 56
Tanzania Environmental Action
        Association (TEACA), 145–146,
        151 n. 2
Tyack, David, 7

Ujamaa, 54–56, 58–59, 63, 113
United Nations Conference on
        Environment and Development
        (UNCED), 35–40, 43 n. 4
Unterhalter, Elaine, 31, 44 n. 7

Vandemoortele, Jan, 89, 92, 105–106

Wagao, Jumanne, 60
Water
    as a commodity, 110, 116, 117, 125,
        126–127
    committees, 125–126
    policies, 113, 114–116, 129
    social-symbolic significance, 124–128,
        130
    see also Furrows
Wright, Marcia, 64 n. 1
Women and Development (WAD), 28–29
Women in Development (WID), 27–28, 31,
        34
World Bank, 32–33, 35–40, 54, 63, 109,
        113–114, 115–116, 123, 125, 129
World Conference on Education for All, 34

Young, Robert, 23 n. 4

SOCIETY AND POLITICS IN AFRICA

Yakubu Saaka, General Editor

This multidisciplinary series publishes monographs and edited volumes that provide innovative approaches to the study and appreciation of contemporary African society. Although we focus mainly on subjects in the social sciences, we will consider manuscripts in the humanities that treat context as a significant aspect of discourse. Within the social sciences, we are looking for not only analytically outstanding studies but, what is more important, ones that may also have significant implications for the formulation and implementation of public policy in Africa. We are especially interested in works that challenge pre-existing hierarchies and paradigms.

For additional information about this series or for the submission of manuscripts, please contact:

Peter Lang Publishing
Acquisitions Department
29 Broadway, 18th Floor
New York, New York 10006

To order other books in this series, please contact our Customer Service Department:

800-770-LANG (within the U.S.)
(212) 647-7706 (outside the U.S.)
(212) 647-7707 FAX

Or browse online by series at:

www.peterlang.com